HIDING IN PLAIN SIGHT

HIDING

IN PLAIN SIGHT

ELUDING THE NAZIS

IN OCCUPIED FRANCE

Sarah Lew Miller and Joyce B. Lazarus

ACADEMY CHICAGO PUBLISHERS

Published in 2012 by
Academy Chicago Publishers
363 West Erie Street
Chicago, Illinois 60654

© 2012 by Sarah Lew Miller and Joyce B. Lazarus

First edition.

Printed and bound in the U.S.A.

Library of Congress Cataloging-in-Publication Data
Miller, Sarah Lew, 1926–
Hiding in plain sight : eluding the Nazis in occupied France /
Sarah Lew Miller and Joyce B. Lazarus.—1st ed.
p. cm.
Includes bibliographical references.
ISBN 978-0-89733-678-9 (hardcover)
1. Miller, Sarah Lew, 1926– 2. Jews—France—Biography. 3. Holocaust,
Jewish (1939–1945)—France—Personal narratives. 4. Jewish children in the
Holocaust—France—Biography. 5. World War (1939–1945)—Personal
narratives, Jewish. 6. France—History—German occupation, 1940–1945.
I. Lazarus, Joyce Block. II. Title.
DS135.F9M556 2012
940.53'18092—dc23
[B]
2012031075

TABLE OF CONTENTS

ACKNOWLEDGMENTS

WE WOULD LIKE TO EXPRESS our appreciation to all those who helped us in the writing and publication of this memoir.

Many thanks to Sarah's relatives who shared with us their recollections, letters and insights, making a valuable contribution to the book: Michel Szlamka, Ava Szlamka, Simone Fiszbin, Claire Weinfeld, Madeleine Laufer and Max Lew.

Thanks to Dr. Diane Afoumado, at the U.S. Holocaust Memorial Museum in Washington, D.C., who provided important documents related to the German occupation of France.

We are very grateful to Dr. Anita Miller and Jordan Miller, to Mary Egan, Zhanna Vaynberg, Rebecca Baumann, Joan Sommers, Rachel Burman and Rachel Brusstar at Academy Chicago Publishers for their support, helpfulness, and hard work in the production of this book.

Lastly, we owe a debt of gratitude to Sarah's children, Rebecca and Gabriel; to mine, Suzanne, Marty and Michael; and to my husband Carl, for their steadfast encouragement, support and love.

PREFACE

SO MUCH HAS ALREADY BEEN WRITTEN about the Vichy years—the "Dark Years"—that it seems at first glance that there may be nothing new to say. There have been countless historical studies, novels, and many award-winning films, such as Marcel Ophuls's *Le Chagrin et la Pitié* (The Sorrow and the Pity, 1969); François Truffaut's *Le Dernier Métro* (*The Last Metro*, 1980); and Louis Malle's *Au Revoir, les Enfants* (*Goodbye, Children*, 1987), to name just a few.

So why now?

It is because I had the good fortune to meet Sarah Miller, a survivor of the Occupation in France, who had a unique story to tell. Her Polish-Jewish immigrant family miraculously survived four years of German occupation, against overwhelming odds. I learned from Sarah Miller about day-to-day life as a teenager in occupied France, living with the ever-present threat of death. She told me how her family of ten had gone into hiding in cities and rural villages scattered around France. They had survived thanks to their own resourcefulness and thanks to assistance given to them by many Christians and by members of the Jewish Resistance. I realized that there was so much about this period that I still wanted to understand, after reading history books and memoirs that left many questions unanswered. I wanted to know whether Jewish life had been able to continue throughout the

Occupation (yes, it had) and how neighbors, French police officers, and strangers had all responded to the persecution of Jews.

Our conversations and correspondence led to the creation of this memoir, *Hiding in Plain Sight: Eluding the Nazis in Occupied France,* which relates the childhood and young adulthood of Sarah Lew Miller (born in 1926) during the years 1932–1948. All events mentioned in this book are true and the characters are real. While family members are given their real names in this narrative, friends, acquaintances, and strangers have been given fictitious names because they have not given us permission to use their names.

While historical studies paint a broad picture of momentous events, they often do not bring to life everyday occurrences and chance encounters that can make the difference between life and death. This is what I wanted to explore with Sarah Miller, as we relived together the years 1932–1948 in first-person narrative form. The memoir is both personal and historical—it is the life of an entire nation—France—and that of one family and their teenage girl Sarah.

During the German occupation of France (1940–1944), nearly 80,000 Jews were murdered, including almost 11,000 children. This memoir tells the story of some who survived the Occupation and also of those who perished during this tragic period.

I read a remarkable story written by Sarah Miller entitled, "Oh, Beautiful Switzerland, How I Remember Thee!" She described her terrifying escape to Switzerland and a young man from the *Sixième,* a Jewish Resistance organization, who had saved her life. The story of heroes—Jewish and non-Jewish—who risked their lives every day and whose acts of bravery and courage are not well known was a story we both felt should be told. As I got to know Sarah's family members through our correspondence, I realized that her siblings and parents, and in particular her mother, showed much valor as well. As we see one family's way of coping with a terrible social and political crisis, we can learn much about ourselves and our own society.

We met each other in a serendipitous way. I had recently published a book called *In the Shadow of Vichy: the Finaly Affair* (Lang, 2008) and had given a copy of it to my cousins Norman Rogoff and Rosalind Guild, who live in a senior residence in Canton, Massachusetts. After finishing it, they donated it to their library and Sarah Miller picked up the book there. I had signed it and written a personal message inside to my cousins. Sarah realized immediately that her own life story was related to the story I had been writing about—Jewish survival during the Vichy period and its aftermath—and she wanted to ask me some questions. Norman Rogoff copied down her e-mail address for me on a small napkin he was holding and we soon began to correspond.

While working on this project together, Sarah Miller and I discovered that we had much in common: her parents and my grandparents were Orthodox Jews from Eastern Europe and their large families both immigrated to Paris. My grandparents knew many hardships, as do all immigrants, but they did not face life-or-death situations on a daily basis, as Sarah's family did. The dream of playing music was very important for Sarah Miller as well as for my parents and for myself as we were growing up. I knew, however, that Sarah Miller's generation had very limited opportunities for women, compared to mine. It is important to highlight the differences between the era of the 1930s and 1940s and that of later generations. Working together has been a creative, fulfilling, and exciting experience. I am very thankful to Sarah Miller for having this opportunity.

—Joyce B. Lazarus, March, 2012

* * *

While watching my children growing up free, happy and without worries, many memories of my youth and my family came to mind. What a different world I grew up in! The need to write my story for them was there, but the courage and the time to begin it? Not yet.

Years later, with the children grown and my husband and I retired, I took a creative writing class at the Jewish Center in Stamford, Connecticut, where we lived. One day our teacher announced that the city of Stamford was sponsoring a writing contest for all ages, and she would like us all to participate. I hesitated, somewhat shy, but suddenly, without hesitation, I sat down at my desk and wrote, "Oh Beautiful Switzerland How I Remember Thee," the saga of a group of Jewish children smuggled into Switzerland during the Holocaust years. Thanks to the French Jewish Resistance group called *La Sixième*, I was one of them.

Sometime later the teacher in our classroom announced proudly that she received notice that her pupil Sarah Miller had won first place in nonfiction. What a nice surprise! Inspired, I began to write on my own. I produced "Remembrance," related to my youth, my family, and the way it was during the Nazi Occupation. I saw that those who read it were touched by it, and they advised me to put it in print for others to read.

I thought about it for a while, but never followed through seriously, until fate came into play. I met Joyce Lazarus by corresponding with her on the computer. I read a book of hers related to France after the war. I had a question. She responded right away with an answer. She also asked me if I had some writings of my own and if so she would like to read them. She did, thus beginning a working relationship and the creation of *Hiding in Plain Sight: Eluding the Nazis in Occupied France*.

—Sarah Lew Miller, March, 2012

CHAPTER 1

DERECZYN, POLAND, 1932–1936

WHEN I LOOK BACK NOW on my childhood and adolescence, I have to marvel at how I survived it all. There were times when I wondered if I would be alive today, in this new century, or if I would still find happiness after seeing the dark side of human nature. I can say that, yes, I still am thrilled at the sight of trees on a lovely spring day, and a sunset reflected on a quiet pond. But there were many dreams I had to abandon along the way. I don't know if the child once inside of me has gone away for good—but if she has, then who did she become?

My childhood ended when I was fourteen, when my family and I began our daily struggle to survive. After Hitler's army conquered France and occupied this country from June 1940 until January 1945, we Jews, especially since we were immigrants, were targeted almost immediately for extermination. We faced the military and political might of Nazi Germany and their willing partner, Vichy France, and we fought against overwhelming odds. As I look back on this battle to survive, I often think about how it changed forever the person I would become and who I am today.

Although I live today in a country free of fear and cruelty, I sometimes find myself returning to a world where decisions and actions so often had life-or-death consequences. How did my family and I live through those long, terrifying years? Perhaps my own journey can help others to understand an era before it has been transformed by myth and legend.

* * *

When I was six years old, living in Poland, I sat in the last row of a large classroom. The one-room school had a blackboard up front, and just above it, a clock. From the back row, I stared hard at the clock and strained to read it. The large and small hands of the clock blurred together. Was it 2:05, or perhaps 1:10? I wanted very much to learn to tell time. Since Jews sat in the back and gentiles in the front at my school, I squinted to read letters and numbers and could not see the pictures or the words, all so far away. I didn't dare to ask the teacher a question. My shyness around teachers kept me from speaking up.

It was 1932. I was the fifth child in my family and I lived in a Polish *shtetl* (a village with a large Jewish population) called Dereczyn, a town that no longer exists. My grandpa had been a well-to-do businessman who lost much of his wealth during the Russian Revolution. He owned a general store in the center of town. When his daughter, my mama, came of age, he went to a yeshiva, the famous Yeshiva of Radin, to look for a husband for her. He picked out my papa, a well-educated man, to be his son-in-law. You might suggest that Mama should have had a say in the matter, to decide whom she would marry. She was a romantic at heart and dreamed a lot about her future. But that was the way matches were made, so she accepted her fate. Besides, her groom turned out to be a handsome young man. So in 1918, my parents, Scheina and Abram, were married.

Papa had been a student all his life and had just become a rabbi. Who would have predicted that he would have to earn his livelihood in business? When Grandpa installed Papa in a leather goods store in Dereczyn, Papa knew nothing about leather goods and even less about working in a business. He could tell you everything about the Torah and how to pray to God, but he was no match for the ruthless dealers who wanted to fleece him. He went on his first business trip to Warsaw and came home with no money and no merchandise. But since Dereczyn didn't need another rabbi, Papa continued to work in his store. Every night, he pored over his prayer books at home.

Our main street was a row of white wooden buildings standing close together: a general store along with a few other stores, a synagogue, several small homes, and, just outside town, two large churches, Russian and Polish. There was a central square where once a week we had market day and farmers brought their fresh produce into town. I can still smell the aromas of cabbage, sour dill pickles, sweet berries, and fresh bread. Wandering musicians played on the town square. A group of gypsies would sometimes camp in our village. These gypsy violinists played melodies that would begin like soft weeping and would suddenly become joyous and wildly exuberant. During summer nights I could hear the sounds of their haunting melodies drifting through my open window. That was when I began to dream that I would become a violinist when I grew up.

I still remember our small wooden house near the center of town. With no electricity, we depended on kerosene lamps and a wood stove, which made our indoor air suffocating. We drew water from a well in the middle of the village to fill our tubs and washed our clothes in a nearby river. Just before Sabbath men and women went to their separate bathhouses. Some Jews had their own land. My uncle's family had a pretty home surrounded by trees on a plot of land with a stream running through it. One day my brothers and sisters and I ran barefoot to his home to escape a big fire close-by. Fires sometimes spread quickly from one wooden house to the next, since they stood so close to each other. We raced down the main street and felt pebbles and rocks scraping our bare feet. We kicked up clouds of dust and didn't stop running until we reached the safety of Uncle's home. Even though my uncle was prosperous in Dereczyn, that didn't mean that he could escape hardship or sadness. His beautiful daughter, my cousin, lay on her couch when we arrived, contorted in a coughing fit. Her bright pink cheeks made her seem healthy, but people told me that rosy cheeks were a dreaded sign of tuberculosis.

Grandpa turned over the management of his store to his daughter and son-in-law, my aunt and uncle, who lived in the same house. He had become sick and depressed ever since the old Russian rubles he had tucked under his mattress had become worthless. My uncle never said a friendly word to us when my brothers and sisters and I would stop by his store. He stood behind the counter, a tall silhouette glancing down at us, a scrawny gang of kids. Was he worried about our asking for candies, or even taking something behind his back? On the wall of his store hung a large poster of a black child holding a shoe in one hand and a shoe brush in another. The child's white teeth sparkled and his twinkling eyes seemed to stare straight at me as I entered the store. An advertisement for shoe polish from a faraway place called America.

I had a boy friend, Chaim, who lived across the street from our house in a large home that had white curtains on the windows and polished furniture. His family kept a goat in his shed and they had a piece of land behind his home. He let me pet his goat and play with him in his garden, looking for pretty stones. We would talk on and on about games, our school and the future. When he asked me what I was going to be when I grew up, I would say with confidence, "I'll be a teacher first and then a violinist." Chaim was going to move to Warsaw to attend college. On Saturdays I watched Chaim enviously as he and his grandpa walked together in their dressy outfits to synagogue. His grandpa wore traditional black clothes with a shiny wide-brimmed black hat.

Grandpa, Uncle, and Papa, along with all the other Jewish men in our town, worked every day except for the Sabbath. They learned the ropes of doing business with gentiles in order to survive. As for us kids, we soon found out that we had to keep to ourselves, to be among Jews. We learned this the hard way when my brother Bernard and his friends decided on one hot summer day to go swimming in a river just outside the town. Many hours later he had not returned. The sun was getting low in the sky. Mama paced back and forth and stopped by our neighbors' homes, asking if they had seen him. *Where could he have gone?* we wondered. Just as the sun was setting, Bernard staggered into our house, out of breath, bruised and bleeding, his pants torn, his *yarmulke* (skullcap) gone. He collapsed onto his bed. A gang of young hoodlums had come upon them by the river, beaten them with rocks and sticks and chased them through the woods, taunting them with their screams of "Jews! Jews!" They ran for their lives. Mama listened in silence for a few moments. Then she screamed, "And your *yarmulke?* You've lost it! How can I buy you another one?" Mama explained later that a poor child without shoes or with torn pants was not as bad as a Jewish boy without a *yarmulke.*

* * *

The police in our town were nasty and corrupt. They came by our house to collect taxes. There were times when business was poor and we had no money to pay them. They then helped themselves to bedcovers, pillows, pots, and pans—anything that they could grab. We were cleaned out of our meager possessions. Sometimes when we knew they were coming, we would hide our blankets and pillows at a neighbor's home for safekeeping.

I don't remember ever seeing any toys in our home. We made up games outside instead. My days revolved around the games my sisters and brothers and I played with our neighbors. My little sister Claire and I played in the dirt with a group of kids, digging for buried treasures. Buttons and stones that were smooth and perfectly round were among our favorite finds but shiny pieces of metal or chips of pottery were even better. One day as we were playing in front of my house, I could not contain my excitement. I told my friends that I had a brand-new baby sister at home. The circle of kids stopped to stare at me in silence, enviously. Then I found a broken spoon in the dirt and let everyone inspect it. "I'm going to hide this spoon so that when my little sister grows up, she'll have a toy to play with." Again the gang looked at me with quiet respect and envy. While Mama was resting in bed with her newborn daughter, a neighbor was baking rolls in our kitchen, and the scent wafted across the road as we continued to play in the dirt.

On my walk home from school each day I would begin to smell warm bread, *latkes* (potato pancakes), and steaming soup, realizing then how hungry I was. While most kids ate lunches in school prepared by their family, I sometimes had no lunch. On those days, I would race home in the middle of the day to grab a *latke* to take back with me to school. I rushed as fast as my legs could carry me. I could smell the hot pancakes even before I reached my front door.

One day I found Mama at home feeding my baby sister Madeleine. The house was strangely quiet. The kitchen had no inviting aromas. Where was Papa? I wondered. Mama tried to explain, sounding tired. "He went away, Sarah, to look for work in France." Since Madeleine had been born, we were now seven children, an ever-growing family. I missed Papa very much and wanted him to return home. I pictured him poring over his prayer book in the evenings, hardly saying a word to my brothers and sisters and me. His quiet presence made me feel safe and secure.

A few weeks later, Mama held up a letter from Papa to show us. "Papa has a job now in Paris, children. He'll soon be sending us some money home. He is working in a Jewish neighborhood store as a *shohet,* a ritual slaughterer of chickens." In a later letter, Papa would write about how he fainted the first time he had slaughtered a chicken and how he had fallen in the chicken's blood.

Since we rarely had milk and our meals had become much smaller, we depended on our neighbors to put a meal on our table. My brother Jacques, only one year older than me and so much more like a twin than an older brother, developed the same strange condition that I had, probably caused by poor nutrition. We felt sudden weakness whenever we exerted ourselves. Some days we felt pain all over and had difficulty walking, but we tried to hide this from our friends.

Seasons followed one another in an orderly rhythm. In the spring we smelled the aroma of baking *matzos* coming from our neighbor's house, as they prepared them for all of us in the village. Bernard, Jacques, Claire and I would stand just outside their doorway to catch the delicious scent drifting on the breeze and to watch villagers bustling about. Our neighbors would help one another when one family had no food. Poor as we were, we would somehow all manage to have a good Passover Seder. I would walk with Mama, carrying a basket, to buy eggs at a farm just out of town. The heavy rains turned our dirt road into mud, and walking to school without getting our legs soaked became a challenge. Summer meant that there were longer days to play outdoors. Fall began for us with the sound of the *shofar* (ram's horn) from our synagogue, ushering in the New Year and shorter, cooler days.

Winters were long and cold and dark, illuminated only by the festival of lights at Hanukkah in December. By the light of kerosene lamps, a group of women would sit in a circle in our house during long winter nights, cleaning and drying goose feathers to make pillows and blankets. We kids were supposed to be in bed, but instead we hid behind curtains to listen to the laughter, gossip and jokes, the tall tales about everyone in our town. At any moment, the grown-ups might discover us spying on them. The danger made it even more exciting, as we huddled together whispering and giggling in the dark room.

Poor as we were, life had its magical moments in Dereczyn. Once we stood in a dark tent. I was tightly holding onto Mama's skirt, listening to voices emanating from a brightly lit stage some distance away. The Yiddish Theater was in town that week. A young couple wearing gaudy makeup and colorful clothes stood in the spotlight on a stage, accompanied by a few musicians. "In a small house, we will live a loving life," they crooned in Yiddish to the audience. "We will have two children. Tell me once more, *Oy!* Tell me once more!"

It was 1936, and my peaceful world was about to be turned upside down. Who could have imagined that I would soon be leaving Dereczyn forever, heading into unknown dangers?

CHAPTER 2

A TRAIN JOURNEY, DECEMBER 1936

LIFE CHANGED SUDDENLY WHEN, in late December 1936, Mama announced that we would be moving to France to be with Papa. With the flurry of activity that week—packing our belongings, finding a home for our dog, helping Mama to fill a bucket with homemade jam, loading a bag with bread and salami—there was hardly enough time to say goodbye to all our friends and relatives. There were cards and letters from my friends that brought tears to my eyes. We gave our small brown dog to the mailman after one last hug. I embraced my girlfriends and Chaim and tried not to cry as Mama put us each in charge of carrying a package, a pillow, a knapsack, or a bucket.

On the train, we marveled at the crisp brown leather seats in our compartment, the electric lights and shiny chrome overhead storage bin for our bags. I was ten years old and this was my first trip outside Dereczyn. I had never before traveled by train and had never seen electric lights before that day. In the excitement of riding a train, I felt the weight of the morning's sadness fall away. Everything around me glowed as in a dream that might soon dissolve.

Mama told us that after five years of struggling in Paris as a ritual slaughterer, Papa had earned enough to support us in his Paris apartment. He had worked hard to make ends meet during those past years, though he would have preferred to study or to find a position as a rabbi. As she spoke, I tried but could not remember Papa's face. All I could think about and wonder about was Paris. What would it be like? I tried to picture Papa standing on the train platform waiting for us but could only see a stranger.

The train trip would take two days. From Warsaw, we had to cross through Poland, Germany, and much of France before reaching Paris. Germany was now in the hands of Adolf Hitler. Since coming to power in 1933, Hitler had spoken about the need to rid the country of Jews and other "undesirables" who were to blame for all of Germany's ills. Some people in Dereczyn had heard about new anti-Jewish laws in Germany and the dangers that Jews faced since the National Socialist party had come to power. In neighboring towns in Poland mobs of hoodlums would often go on rampages, looting and murdering Jews and burning down their homes. Pogroms had swept through villages like ours since time immemorial. Surviving Jews would then bury their dead and try to rebuild, to start life all over. Hitler's tirades about Germany being only for the Aryans—white Christians of a certain ethnic background—sent chills down the spines of my family and friends but sounded like speeches of other tyrants they had always heard about. As we traveled closer to the German border, I pictured the German authorities boarding our train and it made my heart race.

We dozed and slept fitfully on our leather seats as the train lurched and rumbled on through the Polish countryside, belching dirty smoke. Looking from my window into the night, I saw illuminated houses that flew by us at a dizzying speed. Some flickering lights seemed to be falling stars settling on the ground. We reached for our loaf of bread and dipped it into the bucket of jam. Mama handed us slices of salami to appease our hunger.

As we approached the German border, the train jerked and screeched to a halt. Then suddenly two uniformed German guards stomped into the train car, their black gloves and high boots shining. I could see the metallic gleam of guns attached to their belts.

They shouted orders: "Passports! Tickets! Identification papers!" Mama reached into her bag and tried to show no emotion as she handed them to the officer. The Germans glanced at our documents and then back at Mama. "These are not valid papers. You cannot continue on this trip through Germany. You must leave the train now." Not comprehending, or perhaps not wanting to listen, Mama did not move. In broken Polish, one of the Germans repeated his orders more loudly, in a barking voice: "Documents worthless! Off the train immediately! Go back to Poland! "

The eight of us scrambled to collect our possessions and step out on the train platform. Claire and Madeleine began to cry. Bernard and Jacques gazed blankly at me. Mama all at once collected her wits. She confronted the German guards standing in the train station head-on. "We are not going back to Poland. We must go on to France. We must continue. I would rather throw myself under the train with all my children than go back." The border guards stared at her but did not bother to reply. Would this be the end? Would the guards arrest us? I didn't dare breathe. I kept my gaze on the stone platform.

A nun wearing a dark habit suddenly appeared on the platform and walked up to Mama. I could not understand her words but caught the soothing tone of her voice as she whispered something to her. She spoke rapidly to a German officer and motioned to all of us to come with her. Whatever she said to the officer had persuaded him to let us leave with her.

We followed her down dark, deserted streets, covering our faces as best we could against the icy wind. It was about a mile or two until we reached a fortress-like ancient stone monastery surrounded by trees and a high wall. Our legs were numb with cold and we were still trembling with fear. We climbed a narrow staircase, following her into a sparsely furnished room where she said we could stay. It wasn't until we were safely settled on our cots for the night that we could breathe more freely. We realized then how much we had to be grateful for. This nun who was a complete stranger had just rescued us, a family of eight Jews with barely any money or food, from the German authorities. We thanked her profusely and thanked God for our narrow escape. In the dark room, we wondered silently how long we would be stranded in Nazi Germany and how we would ever reach Paris. Soon a deep sleep engulfed us all.

Early the next day we awoke to the sounds of church bells calling the nuns to prayer. Our nun greeted us smiling, with a tray of dark pumpernickel bread, creamy butter and hot tea. Through the narrow windows of our room we could see the courtyard outside where some tall frozen trees swayed a little in the cold breeze. After breakfast, she told us that she knew of a Jewish man living nearby who might be able to help us. Mama and the nun went off to find him, while the rest of us explored the stone corridors and hidden staircases of the monastery. We tried to imagine that we were in a medieval castle and marveled at the muffled voices and the rustle of nuns in their long habits moving through dimly lit rooms. Mama told us later that it had taken a lot of persuasion from the nun before the old Jewish man agreed to open his door to them. Jews in Germany lived in isolation and in terror of Hitler, never knowing if the next knock on the door would be the Gestapo. Our guardian angel had persuaded him to write to the emigration authorities in Warsaw to mail us the missing legal document.

Sure enough, about ten days later the legal paper arrived, and we hugged our dear nun, thanking her for her kindness and help. On January 3, 1937, our train arrived in Paris and we were reunited with Papa, a man I hardly knew. Paris meant, above all else, safety and a chance for a new life. Hitler, meanwhile, was conspiring with Italy and Japan and making plans to take over Austria. The German army would soon spread its tentacles over Europe. In a few short years much of the continent would be engulfed in flames.

CHAPTER 3

A NEW LIFE IN PARIS, 1937

A TALL MAN WITH A REDDISH BEARD stood on the train platform—my papa—and greeted us with a broad smile. Five long years of separation were between us. The Paris Métro rumbled into the station, its jarring, screeching brakes echoing through the tunnel. Strangers jostled each other. From an open train car, grownups, toddlers, and children spilled out onto the platform like water bursting from a dam. Some people looked haggard, others engrossed in private thoughts; their faces betrayed little emotion. I was silent during our walk up the hilly sidewalk through the working class neighborhood, which Papa called the eighteenth *arrondissement*. The white dome of the imposing Sacré-Coeur dominated the hilltop of bustling Montmartre.

On the way to our apartment at 84 Rue Marcadet, we passed street vendors peddling their fruits and vegetables, shouting to passersby to buy their fresh apples and *haricots verts*. I stared at everything, amazed by the variety of produce, the smells and colors, the dizzying crowds that packed our sidewalk. I might just as well have landed on another planet. The apartment itself was a big disappointment: two rather ugly rooms with a kitchenette big enough for one person to stand in. There was cold running water from one faucet and a bathroom outside the apartment down the hallway. Our family would be able to use public showers in the neighborhood, and a *lavoir,* a wash house with sinks and drying racks in separate cubicles for our laundry. More importantly, though, we were going to be together as a family at last.

Our apartment was on the second floor. To reach it, you crossed an enclosed cobblestone courtyard, in the center of which stood an ancient maple. The entranceway to our staircase had no lighting unless you pushed a small button on the wall that operated with a timer. Before I became accustomed to using this button I stumbled blindly on the stairs and banged my head against walls. Already I missed the open sky of Dereczyn, my friends, relatives, and a language I could understand. I could only see myself as an outsider in Paris. I was a quiet child, not rebellious like Hélène and Bernard. My younger sister Claire, however, began at once to show her anxiety about our new surroundings with frequent screams and temper tantrums.

Before long our neighbors complained about us and our crowded household became very tense. Papa would spank Claire when she began to scream. One time I had to stand in front of her to shield her from Papa's anger.

We eventually settled into a routine. Along with my two brothers, Bernard and Jacques, Claire and I took the Métro each day, except the Sabbath, to attend a private school financed by the famous Baron de Hirsch family. We had to get used to riding the Métro for what seemed like hours, as we changed trains along the route. Teeming crowds jostled us as we elbowed our way through cavernous tunnels in the subway. Once we arrived at school, boys and girls went to separate classes and we were served kosher meals. All Jewish holidays were observed. Before entering our classrooms we would line up to have our hands inspected for cleanliness. One day I arrived a few minutes late and the directress looked at me severely. I trembled as I waited for her to inspect my hands. She looked me over and put her hand on my forehead. "You don't look good today, Suzanne." ("Sarah" became "Suzanne" in France.) "I'm sending you back home."

On most days, I would gaze at a small piece of blue sky visible through the high windows next to my desk. I liked to study the patterns of sunlight on desks and children's faces. As much as I wanted to concentrate on what the teacher was saying, I could not understand her French and found myself continually lost. The teacher, an older unmarried woman with dark hair and an unsmiling face, gave her lectures in a voice without inflection. I always hoped that she would not call on me.

Why did we have to leave Dereczyn anyway? I longed for the open sky of the village, my old familiar surroundings and friends. Here I was at ten years old, restless, bored and lonely in school, where children ignored me because of my foreign accent. At recess, as I stood by myself in a corner of the playground, I could hear girls whispering, "Look at that foreign girl! Where is she from?" On other days, some girls would point to my mismatched colored gloves and laugh among themselves. Mama had been too busy with her large brood of kids to help us all dress properly.

Anger welled up in me at my parents for bringing me to Paris. Watching clouds move slowly across the blue sky, I pretended to be a bird flying high, gliding far away from the worn stone walls of my school, my uncaring teacher, and my parents who didn't love me since they had brought me here without even consulting me.

Bernard, Jacques, Claire, and I soon figured out that if we sold our return Métro tickets at the station in the afternoons we would have enough money to buy a delicious pastry at a bakery. As we stood at the Métro entrance, most pedestrians ignored us, but occasionally someone would buy our tickets and even give us a few extra pennies. We would have a long walk home then. It took over an hour. Bernard and Jacques went off together, while Claire and I stopped at several different bakeries and compared every *croissant*, *pain au chocolat* and *éclair* until we had selected one. Saleswomen would lose their patience as we gazed, transfixed, at the many luscious chocolate cakes and cream puffs in the glass cases. Finally,

Claire and I would buy one pastry, break it into two portions and eat it very slowly to savor it during the long walk home.

Sometimes, after school, Bernard would take me for rides on the back seat of his bicycle and we would race through our neighborhood at full speed. Holding on tightly to Bernard's jacket, I laughed and screamed with excitement and fear. He began to pick up French very quickly. Other times, Papa would take me for walks on the long hilly streets toward Montmartre and I never stopped marveling at the mouth-watering foods sold in vendors' stalls: hot French fries in small packets made of folded newspapers, warm *gaufrettes* (waffles) covered in powdered sugar. Once my father bought me a banana and told me it was delicious. I refused to try it. It looked strange and disgusting. "You can give it to Claire, if you like," I suggested. In his frustration Papa spanked me. I was just as disgusted by the sight of cooked chestnuts being sold on street corners. I had heard once, back in Poland, that they were used to make glue. Weren't these chestnuts a kind of poison?

July 14, Bastille Day in our new country, took us all by surprise. The cafés and restaurants on Rue Marcadet were festooned with strings of colored lights, illuminating the neighborhood as the summer sky slowly darkened. Crowds filled the streets and music wafted through the pleasant night air as a breeze stirred trees just outside our window. My older brothers, Claire, and I found ourselves following a sea of neighbors, spilling out of nearby apartment houses, all moving toward the source of the music. Just around the corner, a group of street musicians were playing dance music. Some couples danced in the middle of the street, while others stood by, joking and laughing. One café was having a song contest and the café owners invited passersby to participate. A neighbor was crooning a popular song: "*Viens au Bal de l'Amour. Profitons des beaux jours. Le temps passe, s'envole et ne revient pas.*" (Come to the Dance of Love. Let's enjoy the good times. Time passes, flies away, and does not return.)

Further down the street some adults were organizing games for children. A middle-aged man announced a potato sack race and began helping children to step into long, tan canvas bags. It was impossible to stay on the sidelines. Friendly crowds pushed us towards the other children who were jumping up and down with excitement. Before we knew what had happened, the four of us were hopping wildly in our sacks and squealing with laughter as we raced to the finish line, where someone showered us with candies. On our way back to the apartment later that night, I sang songs I had overheard in the cafés. Mama was cleaning up in the kitchen, too busy to enjoy the excitement. She stared at our glowing faces with wonder.

Not long after we had settled into our new lives in Paris, Mama discovered that she was pregnant. Mama and Papa worried about where in Paris she should go to give birth. Would a public hospital be the right place for a Jewish woman? What about the Rothschild Hospital, a public hospital with a very good reputation?

At around this time, my older sisters Paulette and Hélène had some tense conversations with Mama about her pregnancy, which I did not really understand. Mama looked worried, but she did not share her thoughts with Claire or me. For Papa and Mama, whatever happened was God's will.

Weekdays were very disorganized and rushed; we did not have much time to relax. On Fridays, however, the whole family went to the two bathhouses, and Hélène and Paulette helped Mama to clean the apartment. The table was set for Sabbath dinner and the apartment was filled with the delicious aroma of chicken soup. After dinner, Papa, at ease now, would tell us Bible stories that filled my imagination with fantastic tales of people who seemed somehow very human. I believed them and loved them all.

CHAPTER 4

AT HOME IN PARIS, 1938

IN 1938, MY FAMILY MOVED to 80 Rue Doudeauville, in the same eighteenth *arrondissement*. Our new apartment was larger and had plenty of light, not just from windows, but also from a glass ceiling over the living room. We learned that we were the first tenants to occupy the building, which had been used previously as a factory. Our main complaint with the new apartment was that it had no heating system, just a small coal heater that we kept in the bedroom area. In the winter it was freezing cold and in the summer very hot. We had a gas range in the kitchen for cooking and a bathroom with cold running water in the hallway. We shared this bathroom with other tenants.

To get into the building you had to ring a bell, and a *concierge* (building caretaker) would check your names to let you in. You would then walk through a dark hallway to stairs on the left that led up to three or four floors of apartments. If you walked straight ahead, instead of taking the stairs, you would come to an enclosed courtyard with an expanse of open sky. In one corner of the courtyard was a door to the synagogue.

Papa was hired as a Hebrew teacher for this synagogue. He would prepare boys for their *bar mitzvah* and also act as *shamas* (guardian) of the synagogue. It was Papa who would blow the *shofar* (ram's horn) announcing the beginning of the New Year for our High Holy Days. The sound of his voice filtering through this ancient instrument had a spiritual quality that filled me with awe.

My family soon settled into the Jewish community, a complete world in itself that was removed from the larger worlds of Paris and the rest of France. For example, our neighborhood had small Jewish stores which sold kosher meat such as delicious salamis that hung from the ceiling and freshly slaughtered kosher chickens. There were bakeries with bagels and cakes galore, and grocery stores where the owner knew us all by name. In nearby non-Jewish bakeries, freshly baked *croissants, éclairs* and *baguettes* displayed on open shelves tempted us with their heavenly aroma. Mama would sometimes stop there to pick up day-old *croissants* at a reduced price. Although she barely spoke a word of French, Mama was at home in our Yiddish-speaking neighborhood where she could navigate easily in stores. She had little interaction with non-Jews, other than exchanging a smile or a simple greeting.

Papa liked to socialize with members of his *shul* (synagogue). Sometimes he invited a few friends over to chat about politics and current events. I would catch their laughter in the living room as they sipped a glass of schnapps.

With seven growing children and a baby on the way, I knew it was not easy for Mama and Papa to make ends meet. Nevertheless, Mama managed to prepare an additional meal every Wednesday evening for a young Yeshiva student named Yaron. He was a skinny young man of about eighteen who never looked at us kids or spoke a word to us. Throughout dinner he kept his head down and remained silent. After the meals, though, I'd hear him say "Thank you very much" to Mama before he left. Mama later explained that he had fled Poland to avoid being drafted into the Polish army, which exploited soldiers mercilessly. Each day of the week, Yaron was given a meal from a different family in our neighborhood. Without these meals, he would not have survived.

My two older sisters Hélène and Paulette did not go to school in Paris; instead, they went right away to work in a garment factory. After long days of sewing during the week, they had to bring home pants and shirts to mend during their evening hours. There was no time left for them to enjoy themselves with friends. The money that they earned at their sweatshop all went to feed our family. There were sparks and soon a strong electric current between Paulette and Hélène as they grew into young adults. Paulette was indisputably more beautiful, and as a result, the apple of Papa's eye. Hélène never got over the attention shown to our sister, the admiring glances of boys, and all the flattering comments surrounding Paulette. It did not seem fair to her that Paulette, with her beautiful braids wrapped around her head, could charm people by merely glancing their way.

My life was easier than that of Paulette and Hélène. True, I had school and homework, but I began to enjoy learning. The Hirsch School, while teaching Jewish Studies, put French ahead of all other subjects. Our school usually beat the public schools in our annual neighborhood competitions. I began to master French quickly and got consistently good grades. My teacher, Mademoiselle Lazare, who had looked severe and intimidating a few months before, began to smile at me and compliment me on my French compositions.

After a short time in Paris, I earned the nickname of "smiley" because of my sunny disposition. Some girls at my school began to ignore my foreign accent and we soon developed strong friendships. There was free time in the afternoons for fun with friends, both Jewish and non-Jewish, and with my brothers and younger sisters. The enclosed courtyard behind my apartment house became our preferred meeting place after school for games.

My dream of playing a musical instrument became a reality, too. Although it was the piano and not my favorite instrument, the violin. Mama had visited an elderly Jewish woman in our neighborhood and when she entered her apartment, she was amazed to hear lovely piano music coming from the living room. A young lady, my neighbor's granddaughter, was playing a classical piece very artistically. Mama thought of my love of music and asked her neighbor a favor: would she permit her granddaughter to give me piano lessons? The answer was yes! I soon began weekly lessons.

Paris was a new world that never stopped filling me with wonder. It was more exciting than anything I could have imagined back home in Dereczyn. Bernard, Jacques, Claire, and I would take long walks to explore the neighborhood and we quickly discovered a long boulevard, Boulevard Magenta, which had many large department stores. Our favorite store was Monoprix, with three or more floors of glittering merchandise of every kind. What we liked to do most of all was to take the shiny escalator up to the top floor and then back down again. Claire and I would say to our brothers, "Can we go along with you two? Please let us!" We would then follow them anywhere and do anything they proposed. The four of us kept riding the escalator, all the while laughing and joking in loud voices, until the store manager, in exasperation, finally threw us all out of the store.

Then there were all the movie theaters in Paris. Our gang would stare longingly at posters advertising the latest films at Cinema Rex and we would wish we had enough money to see the new movie. Once, we came up with a wild plan to make it happen. Jacques paid the full cost of admission and went into the theater, while the rest of us walked to the side street just behind the theater and waited. After a few minutes, Jacques opened the exit door and the three of us crept into the theater like thieves to see the movie.

We dreamt up other mischievous games in the neighborhood that our parents never found out about. My older brothers led the way and Claire and I willingly followed whatever they did.

Jacques and Bernard would take turns ringing doorbells at different apartment houses just to watch the *concierge* come to the door, while we all hid around the corner. Sometimes the *concierge* would step outside and look around, and seeing no one, would yell, "*Des sauvages! Ces enfants sont de petits sauvages!*" (Savages! These kids are little savages!) Crouching behind the wall of a nearby building, we would cover our mouths to keep from laughing out loud.

On Sundays, when we had free time, my brothers, Claire, and I would sometimes follow the bustling Boulevard Barbès to the end of the Métro line to Porte de Clignancourt. It was an exhausting walk, but worth every step. For us it was a road to paradise. When we arrived there we found the *Marché aux Puces* (Flea Market), a magical place filled with every imaginable type of merchandise displayed on tables and on the ground. Vendors loudly hawked their goods, each one offering the "best deal ever" for shiny combs, mirrors, hats, toys and household items. Not having any money in our pockets, we stared at the colorful displays and basked in the excitement, wondering why customers did not snatch up the combs and mirrors at such bargain prices. I read the first pages of comic books piled high on the ground, and was soon immersed in the adventures of fantastic characters. Dancers and acrobats performed in the middle of the square, accompanied by violinists and accordionists. We squeezed between the grown-ups and always found a place to sit on the ground near the front of the square. The musicians and dancers left old hats on the ground, hoping the public would reward their talents with a mountain of coins and bills.

On other Sundays, we would take a left turn from Rue Doudeauville towards Boulevard de Rochechouart, walking toward Place Pigalle. It was a very wide boulevard where we enjoyed people-watching. We saw elegantly dressed tourists, young couples walking arm-in-arm, and beggars crouching near the storefronts. Once or twice a year, the boulevard was closed to vehicles and became transformed overnight into a circus, with music, performances, clowns, games, and food stands. A week later, the magic would abruptly vanish, leaving behind torn ribbons, prizes, and posters of clowns all strewn about on the street.

Looking back on that summer of 1938, I think I overheard some of Mama and Papa's whispered conversations in the evening about the alarming state of events in Europe: Germany's invasion and annexation of Austria, the terrible racial laws in Germany that stripped Jews of their civil rights, their jobs, and their right to an education. If I did overhear them, I certainly did not see the connection between those events in faraway Germany and our present lives in peaceful Paris. My family surrounded me like a solid fortress, and, being twelve years old, I assumed that this world would always continue.

Rarely did any of us visit Paris neighborhoods far beyond the one where we lived and where I went to school. However, this changed one day when I came down with severe tonsillitis. Papa, towering over me, held my hand tightly as we rode the Métro to Rothschild Hospital. The hospital seemed at first like a beautiful building with high ceilings and gleaming white walls. As we walked down the hallway, however, the strong smell of alcohol and the strange sight of so many doctors and nurses in white uniforms overwhelmed me and I began to cry uncontrollably. Two nurses came running toward me and firmly took my hand from Papa as they led me upstairs. Before I knew what had happened, I woke up with a very sore throat in frightening surroundings: white curtains draped around my bed like ghosts, sounds of low voices everywhere and of metal scraping against bedposts. I tossed and turned in bed until at last daylight filled the room and Papa came to take me home. Back in my own apartment, I felt proud to be the center of so much attention and excited to be eating a bowl of ice cream—a real treat.

My family's other big experience in the world outside our Jewish neighborhood came in August of 1938, when Mama checked into a public hospital to give birth to my baby brother Max. In spite of everyone's misgivings about Mama going to a non-Jewish doctor in a French hospital, we all instantly fell in love with the new baby she brought home. He had a serious little face with soft brown eyes shaped like almonds and a full head of hair. We did not imagine then that this new child would be coming into such a frightening world. Who could have guessed that our "safe" haven would be the eye of a storm, soon after France declared war on Germany one year later?

CHAPTER 5

RUMBLINGS OF WAR,
1938–1939

THE ARRIVAL OF MY BABY BROTHER Max brought excitement and happiness to my family. The walls of our crowded apartment on Rue Doudeauville echoed with baby cries, soothing voices of sisters rocking him in their arms, chuckles and peals of laughter at each new surprise: Max's first smile, his cooing and playfulness, his first crawl. Each of us had a chance to hold him and to feed him, to give Mama a rest. The biggest transformation in our family was the change in Papa. Up until now a serious, towering presence of a man who did not show emotion and who did not hug me or my older siblings, Papa to me was quiet, reflective, often engrossed in his prayer book and in Jewish newspapers. We never discussed God or the Bible with Papa. Everything was to be accepted just as it was written, without question. Mama once told me that he had become orphaned as a very young child and had been sent to a yeshiva, far from the comforts of a loving family. Now I watched with envy as Papa coaxed Max to eat with amusing little coin games and made loving, cooing sounds that made Max smile. My Papa who had been absent for so many years of my early childhood became a doting, devoted papa to his youngest child.

As I became more settled in our adopted country, I spent less time thinking about our old town in Poland and instead enjoyed my new friendships. We lived far from the Hirsch School, but a few friends from school and another from my apartment house would sometimes meet me in my enclosed courtyard to talk and play games. Chantal, a non-Jewish friend who lived one floor below me, joined Claire and me for games there. We chatted on and on about our teachers, boys, and plans for the future. I told them about my plans to become a teacher and to take violin lessons. My school friend Viviane said that she wanted to go into her parents' business when she grew up.

All around us, as we laughed and chatted, we were being observed by neighbors who looked at us from their windows facing the courtyard. Madame Relman, a Jewish lady from Romania whose apartment across the courtyard faced mine, was very friendly and talkative and gave us sweets whenever we stopped by to see her. On another side of the building, an old man observed us from behind the iron bars on his window. He smoked cigarettes and sometimes sounded drunk when he spoke to us. We could not understand what he said and we were afraid of him. On a third side of the courtyard, from a basement window, a small, pale, sad-looking boy of about five years old peered at us from behind bars. He was standing on a chair watching us, and we saw from his haunted gaze that he was lonely and miserable. With his window tightly closed, we had no way to communicate with him. We could only stare at one another. I guessed that his parents were both working all day and had no one at home to take care of him.

During a school holiday, Viviane invited me over to her apartment at Place de la République. When she unlocked her door, I was suddenly transported to a beautiful new world. Her spacious, bright living room had polished mahogany chairs covered with silk fabric, floor-to-ceiling bookcases, and a long buffet table. Oriental tapestries adorned the oak floors, and in the dining area, a crystal chandelier hung from the high ceiling. From a vase of fresh flowers on the dining room table, a sweet scent wafted toward me. I tried not to show my amazement, but could not help but whisper, "*Que c'est beau, Viviane!*" (How beautiful it is, Viviane!) over and over as we walked around. The kitchen had a faucet with hot and cold running water and a white porcelain basin. My favorite part of the apartment was Viviane's own bedroom, just for herself, decorated with pastel fabrics, with her own private bathroom and—I could scarcely believe this—a flush toilet and hot running water in the bathtub. We stayed in her room with the door closed, so that we could share our secrets until late in the afternoon.

One Saturday morning I stayed in bed late, chatting with Claire, who shared a bed with me. The apartment was quiet. The men of our house were already at synagogue and Mama had also gone there that day with Max. Then I heard a knock at the door. Claire and I looked at each other, wondering who it might be. To my surprise, Viviane was standing in the doorway. "I came to visit you, Sarah. It must be fun to be surrounded by all your brothers and sisters." Viviane walked right into my messy bedroom and sat down on my bed, wiping her eyes. She did not seem to notice anything around her—neither the plain furniture, nor the bare walls, nor the disarray. At once she began to pour out her heart: "I've just lost my only brother, Sarah. He has decided to marry Elisabeth. Do you remember that girl I told you about, whom I despise? " She paused for a moment. Viviane, a poor little rich girl, was lonely much of the time. Her parents were never home. They worked long hours at their successful business. I put my arm around Viviane as she covered her face to hide her tears.

My older sisters, Hélène and Paulette, now twenty and eighteen years old, were gone for most of the week, since they worked long hours at a garment factory. They mended pants in the evenings and cleaned the apartment with Mama on Fridays. Life was hard for them. On weekends, however, they became young again. Hélène loved to read, like me, and had a pretty singing voice. I would hear her singing in the apartment on Saturday mornings as she got dressed. Paulette and Hélène went out a lot together with their friends and sometimes invited boyfriends to our apartment.

One tall, dark-haired young man, Hélène's boyfriend, spoke in a soft voice with a Yiddish accent. He too was a recent immigrant from Poland.

Every few weeks, Hélène and Paulette carried the family laundry to the *lavoir* (wash house) in the neighborhood, where they spent the whole day washing our clothes. It was my job to bring them lunch. The wash house was an ugly stone structure. They paid a fee to use a sink in a large room where all around us tired-looking women of all ages were busy laundering mountains of clothes. My sisters also rented a cubicle for drying the clothes. Each little room, accessible with a key, consisted of built-in metal bars instead of walls. I guessed it was designed to safeguard our clothing and to dry it easily, but to me, the drab cubicles looked like rows of prison cells. The combined smells of dampness, mold, and strong ammonia detergent were overpowering, and the dim light overhead depressed me. When I stepped outside I always took a deep breath and felt sudden relief.

On Friday afternoons, we all went to the men's and women's bathhouses nearby. Claire and I shared a shower stall and scrubbed each other, all the while laughing and gabbing. On several occasions we both screamed in terror at a man's face that suddenly appeared over the top of our enclosure. He was peering down at us naked in our shower. As we held each other in panic the terrifying face vanished just as suddenly as it had first shown itself. We continued to wash before leaving the bathhouse, but we did so quickly and without laughing. I wondered why no one stopped him.

One evening I found Mama and Papa listening intently to a radio broadcast. I could hear a guttural, barking German voice, followed by the voice of a French translator. The radio distorted the sounds and gave them an eerie quality. Adolf Hitler was addressing Parliament: "If the international Jewish financiers in and outside Europe succeed in plunging nations once more into a world war, the result will not be the victory of Bolsheviks and thus the victory of Jews, but the annihilation of the Jewish race in Europe!" Papa bent his head down with a pained expression on his face that frightened me, although the words on the radio did not make any sense to me.

CHAPTER 6

OUTBREAK OF WORLD WAR II, 1939

MAMA AND PAPA LISTENED to radio broadcasts almost every evening now and spoke to each other in low, concerned voices. Our teachers at school had told us about Crystal Night, which occurred in Germany on November 10, 1938. Angry mobs of civilians, along with Nazi Stormtroopers, had murdered a hundred Jews, attacked and deported tens of thousands more, ransacked their homes, stores, and businesses, and torched more than a thousand synagogues. While this was taking place, the German police stood idly by. There was no telling what fate awaited the Jewish people in Europe. The newspapers brought nothing but chilling news: Nazi Germany annexed Austria in March of 1938 and western Czechoslovakia in September of that same year. Hitler broke his non-aggression treaty with Poland and signed a new pact with Russia. Mademoiselle Bloch, my history teacher, told us that Prime Minister Léon Blum had been right to warn France of the rising threat of Nazism, and to accelerate France's arms production. Unfortunately, Prime Minister Daladier, who replaced Blum, was listening to pacifists and defeatists in Parliament and was not preparing the country for war. It seemed as though France was still traumatized from World War I and was not ready to take Hitler seriously.

My family was having its own drama: Hélène was in love with a young Polish immigrant who often came to our apartment.

He told her he was joining the Foreign Legion and asked her to wait for him. He would return in a few years, become a French citizen and marry her. Papa disapproved of this match and the two of them argued in the evenings. "Hélène, he is poor, he is not for you. What kind of future will you have?" he would say. I did not hear Hélène's tearful response but could feel tensions rising in our crowded apartment.

Paulette and Hélène went one day to a large communist demonstration on Boulevard Barbès. It was their first experience at a political rally. Because of our family's immigrant status, we had tried to keep to ourselves as much as possible and did not usually venture into political demonstrations. In our small Jewish neighborhood, we had always felt secure and insulated from the larger world. Foreigners were excluded from rights that French citizens took for granted: subsidized apartments, monthly benefits for large families, and scholarships for bright children. My youngest sister Madeleine was doing very well in school; her teacher had recently told Mama that she was one of the best students. We knew, however, that she would not be eligible for a scholarship.

Hélène and Paulette did not return home that evening until late; Mama and Papa had begun to grow anxious. When they finally came into the apartment, Hélène ran to her bedroom crying and closed the door. Paulette tried to explain what had happened. "We were in an immense crowd of men and women of all ages, some with children, all shouting, 'To the final battle!' I have never seen so many people in the streets. They were singing and chanting slogans. My French was not good enough so I asked Hélène in Yiddish what it was all about. We never did find out the answer, because a nearby demonstrator overheard us and suddenly grabbed Hélène by the hair. He screamed at us, 'Dirty Jews!' All I could do was pull Hélène away as we elbowed our way through the agitated crowd." After listening in silence for a few minutes, Mama put her arms around Paulette. Papa said that the growing influx of Jews in France escaping from Germany and Eastern Europe was stirring up anti-Semitism. Léon Blum was being blamed for driving the country towards a "Jewish War" that the French people did not want. Papa thought the economic crisis was the real cause of their hatred of Jews. Blum was a scapegoat for everything going wrong in France. After my sisters' ordeal none of us ever attended another rally. We knew that as foreigners, if we called attention to ourselves, we might be sent back to Poland.

By August of 1939 we all knew that France and England would soon declare war on Germany. It was just a matter of weeks. The principal of our school decided to take us students with our teachers to a beach resort in Normandy for safety. Viviane, Claire, a school friend named Rosa, and I were together for two weeks, trying to enjoy ourselves but feeling anxious. In the evenings, our teachers took turns entertaining us with books they read aloud. I ironed shirts for boys to wear for Friday night Sabbath dinner. As we laughed during shared kitchen chores, the war began to seem remote. We were children again for a few days. At other times, though, I caught my teachers reading newspapers aloud together and overheard them whispering about what might happen to our school when war broke out. In spite of the clear blue sky and warm sunlight on the Normandy beach all week, kids and teachers couldn't bring themselves to organize games. The two weeks came to a close much too quickly and we returned to Paris to face whatever awaited us. My friends and I hugged each other and wept as we parted.

September of 1939 was like a long bad dream. I imagined that I would wake up at any moment and return to my bike rides with Bernard and to movie escapades with Claire and Jacques. On other days it felt as though years had passed since the carefree days of just a few months before. On September 4, one of my teachers held up a newspaper with the screaming black headline, "War with Germany." Two teachers put their heads on each other's shoulders and began to weep. Our air raids began almost immediately. Everyone's greatest fear was that Germany might drop gas bombs on Paris. It must have been a terror France had felt ever since World War I. We were given one gas mask thanks to Max. As the only family member born in France, little Max alone had French citizenship. The whole family was eligible to be evacuated out of Paris to Brittany because of Max's status. After the first alert, some women, children, and older people left Paris, but Papa said he did not want us to leave the city.

One day, the shrill, deafening wail of an air raid siren sent a chill down my back. Lights went out all over Paris. The city stopped instantly in its tracks and traffic screeched to a halt. We scrambled downstairs into the basement of our apartment building, holding small flashlights. Papa carried Max in his arms and tried to calm him with his gentle voice. The rest of us put wet napkins over our faces to protect us against a gas attack. The basement smelled of mold and charcoal. In some places parts of the wall were crumbling and we squinted to see where we were walking among chunks of concrete in the obscurity. The cellar was clammy and dirty; it was hard to breathe with so many residents packed into a narrow space. One boy did not stop screaming, "Help! I'm going to die!" He pushed his way through the crowd with a wet napkin on his face. He apparently thought he was inhaling gas and felt as though he were being poisoned. It was only the combined foul odors of mold, dust, and mildew. The crying boy was searching for his family; he had become separated from them in the panic. My family huddled together quietly in a corner until the end of the alert, when a short siren sounded "All clear."

With France now fully engaged in war with Germany, Mama and Papa spent every evening in front of the radio, listening intently to war news. From their tone and knitted brows, we kids gathered that Hitler's army was advancing. During one of these broadcasts, we heard Prime Minister Paul Reynaud announce that all German nationals living in France would be sent to special camps: "Measures have been taken. . . concerning the surveillance of German nationals for reasons of national security." Papa said that this was a clear violation of the right of asylum that France had established centuries ago. The majority of these German nationals were Jews who had fled Nazism, only to be treated as criminals in their adopted homeland. Now they were being hunted down and interned in camps by the French government. What would happen to all of us, as foreigners? No one could feel safe anymore in France.

Yet things were still bearable and life went on as before for us kids. Bernard, Jacques, Claire, and I went to school each week and tried to forget our worries by playing games. Teachers began each day with an announcement about the progress of French troops and we recited a prayer for their safety. Having a routine kept us from thinking too much about war.

On Friday evenings, we tried our best to have a festive Sabbath meal. We were all together as before, but the mood at our dinner table had become more somber. If the Germans arrived in Paris, where would we go? Where would we hide? Papa's gaze had become more brooding, his silences longer. I suddenly pictured him as he had been last year—a different man altogether. On one particular afternoon the previous October, Claire and I had brought him a food package prepared by Mama. He was in his *sukkah*, the small outdoor structure covered with fruits and grapevines for the holiday of Sukkot. It was a long walk down the boulevard to the far end of our neighborhood. As we approached him, we heard him chatting merrily with a few men around him, relaxing with a glass of wine or perhaps schnapps. He had turned and greeted us with a broad grin and laughing eyes. I had not seen those eyes or that smile in many months.

CHAPTER 7

FRANCE'S DEFEAT, JUNE 1940

"FRANCE HAS LOST THE WAR!" Over and over I heard this phrase spoken by teachers, friends at school and my family. I repeated it to myself but still could not make sense of it or believe it. France was defeated. How could this be true?

The French army was overrun as a German *blitzkrieg* had advanced across the northern border through Belgium, taking the French completely by surprise. Hitler's army was marching rapidly toward Paris at that very moment. It was June, 1940. I saw the terror in my teachers' faces and I shivered with fear. Still, I kept silent and tried to imagine what life would be like in the coming days and months. Rumors and news, panic and confusion were all mixed together, so that it was impossible to understand what was really happening.

Just outside my apartment house, groups of neighbors and friends stood huddled together in the courtyard, trying to digest the terrible news. Some Jewish neighbors who were French citizens felt confident that French laws would protect them against arrests. Others said they heard rumors that all Jews would soon be sent to "work camps" in Eastern Europe until the end of the war. We had already seen German nationals arrested and interned in special camps. Who could say where these camps were in Eastern Europe or what they really were? Many neighbors had started to pack and were speaking in whispers of leaving Paris immediately for the countryside. Everyone was terrified of German bombs, which might have fallen on Paris at any time. Papa looked for solace in his prayers. He sat pensively in the dining room while Mama went outside to speak to everyone, to find out how others were planning to hide or escape. She put some money from Papa's salary into a hiding place, to have it ready for an escape or an emergency.

Food rationing soon began in earnest. As food became scarcer, we kids did not have as much energy as we used to and we had trouble concentrating in class. Our teachers became distracted as well, once the news of France's defeat began to sink in. They spoke in lower tones and did not discipline unruly students as before. Every morning, they distributed to all of us some multi-vitamin biscuits and forced us to swallow a spoonful of foul-tasting fish oil. In spite of this unpleasant daily ritual, I still looked forward to school each day. Schoolwork helped to keep me busy and even homework was a way of forgetting depressing war news for a few hours.

Our evenings with Mama and Papa were spent sitting near the radio—it had an irresistible magnetic power over us. The crackling voices, broken up by static, spoke of France's "honorable fight" and "heroism."

Mama, ever the resourceful person, said that we could not all stay there in Paris. It was getting more dangerous every day. Within days or weeks Hitler's army would be marching into the capital. Mama feared that the Germans would arrest all young men, especially Jews, and immediately send them to forced labor camps. Since Bernard was the oldest boy in the family and a strong, healthy teenager of seventeen, it seemed that he had the best chance of all of us to escape to the countryside. We did not have the resources for our whole family to leave the city at once. So Mama gave Bernard a small packet of money and told him to pack a small suitcase and to leave Paris the next day. He would look for work on a farm in one of the villages south of the city, far from combat and warfare. At least we could rest assured that all of us would not fall into the clutches of the Germans when they arrived at our apartment house. He packed some clothes, food, and water and barely had time to hug us or to say goodbye early the next morning when he left on his bicycle. We did not know then that Bernard would be joining millions of other panicky and anxious men, women, and children of all ages clogging every road leading out of Paris, all fleeing the approaching German army.

Imagine our astonishment when five days later, a thin, haggard Bernard showed up in our doorway and immediately collapsed on the floor of the apartment. He slept for an entire day and after drinking and eating a little, his first food in three days, Bernard slowly began to tell us about his long ordeal. The roads leading out of Paris had become rivers of refugees—grown-ups, children, and the elderly—riding in cars, on bicycles, or walking, all gripped by panic as they struggled to escape from Paris, ahead of the advancing German army. Some were carrying bundles of clothes on their backs and their arms were weighed down by bags of food. Still others, wealthier Parisians, had furniture piled on top of cars. More and more people joined the long exodus. They walked for days, many without food or water in the June heat. Parents were carrying their tired children; elderly relatives who could not walk were riding in makeshift carts. Gasoline soon ran out and many abandoned their cars and their meager possessions en route.

Bernard continued: "Throughout the day and night you could hear children crying and see sick people lying along the sides of roads. In nearby towns, not a single room was available in a hotel or inn. At night I saw some people sleeping on the floors of cafés or in the fields. All of us kept looking up at the sky with terror as war planes whizzed by. Who knew if they were French or German planes about to bomb us? We were easy targets. Every once in a while you heard an explosion in the distance, and saw dark smoke rising on the horizon. There were bodies of people lying in nearby fields—those who had died of exhaustion, sudden illness, or who had perhaps been hit by a bomb. I could not bring myself to look at them closely.

"I rode as hard as I could and ran out of food after the first day. Luckily I found a stream near the side of the road where I stopped to drink a little water. But by the second night without sleep, I finally collapsed at the side of the road. It was impossible to keep my eyes open anymore. I don't remember how long I slept, perhaps three or four hours, until dawn. All I knew was that when I opened my eyes, my bicycle was gone. It was stolen. Along with my bicycle, I lost all my money, clothes, possessions, everything. It was horrible, like a terrible nightmare. I had to walk all the way back to Paris without any food, a three-day hike. I almost fainted several times from the heat and from hunger."

Bernard fell silent. I saw in his eyes a look I did not recognize. Was it despair, depression, or exhaustion? It was as though Bernard had aged in the past five days and had grown all at once into an older man. He had become transformed into a person we did not know.

One evening later in June, as we sat listening to a news broadcast on the radio, we heard for the first time the voice of a very old man. He sounded like a grandfather when he announced solemnly that he was assuming leadership of the French government, and he then added: "I'm giving to France the gift of myself, to ease France's suffering." Mama and Papa said that this man, named Maréchal Pétain, had apparently been a great war hero from World War I. Perhaps he would help to defend France from the Nazis. Pétain spoke in his gravelly, broken voice: "Our army has fought with a heroism worthy of its long military traditions against an enemy that is superior in number and in weapons. . . It has been an honorable fight. It is with a heavy heart that I say to you today that the fighting must stop. . . May all Frenchmen rally to the government over which I preside during this difficult ordeal. . . and listen only to the faith they have in the destiny of the fatherland."

By this time, most people thought that an armistice was the only possible outcome of the French military defeat. We could only hope that our adopted country would somehow be spared the misery, destruction, and persecutions of other occupied countries in Europe such as Poland, Belgium, and the Netherlands. France was to be divided into German-occupied territory in the north and west and a "free zone" in the southern and eastern third of the country. The new French government would now have its capital in the town of Vichy in central France.

The reality of German occupation began to hit home in the following few months, when anti-Jewish laws were passed very rapidly, starting in October. First, citizenship was taken away from all Jews who had become French citizens since 1927. Then the ban against racism and anti-Semitic speech was removed. Jews living in the occupied zone had to register at the police station, to have the word "*Juif*" (Jew) stamped on their identification cards. With this census, it felt as though the police were observing our every move. Then Jews were forbidden to work for the government or to engage in professions such as journalism, theater, radio, or education. Before we knew what was happening, we learned that all foreign Jews were being rounded up and sent to internment camps. That meant that any day, German or French police might show up at our front door to arrest us. All our efforts to leave Poland, which had brought us to Paris, became futile when we found ourselves at the center of a new storm, more vulnerable than ever before.

I walked by Cinema Rex after school one afternoon and saw, to my horror, a poster for the latest film. The poster had a large caricature of a Jew with a long, hooked nose and an evil sneer. French movies were suddenly a propaganda tool of the Nazis!

What had become of the Paris I knew just a few months before? I stared at Parisians strolling by on the boulevard as if I had never really noticed them before. Were they my neighbors and friends or had they become my enemies? Would they report me to the police?

Paulette and a few of her friends strolled down Boulevard Magenta one Sunday and suddenly came upon a group of German soldiers in Nazi uniforms. The soldiers were joking with each other and slapping each other on the back. When they spotted Paulette and her friends, they tipped their caps and began to flirt in broken French with them. "*Mesdemoiselles très belles!*" They wanted to stay with the girls to chat a little longer. Paulette said all at once without thinking, "You should not talk to us. We are Jewish girls!" One soldier quickly answered with a broad smile, "But that's not possible. The Jews are all *kaput* (finished, dead)." Paulette and her friends could barely conceal their horror as they rushed away. She was still shaking when she later told us about their encounter.

In April of 1941, my family gathered in our synagogue for a small private wedding ceremony. My sister Hélène, twenty-two years old, wore a simple suit and did not carry a bouquet of flowers. She silently wiped her tears away as she signed the wedding *ketubah* (contract) with her groom, Jack, aged thirty-five. Hélène and Jack had an arranged marriage, in the tradition of Mama and Papa. Jack was a French citizen and a prominent businessman in the city of Nevers, in Burgundy. He was well respected and liked by both Jews and non-Jews in his hometown. Right after they signed their papers, Hélène and Jack left Paris. It was good to know that they would be far from the eyes of German policemen who were everywhere in the streets of Paris. As I saw them leave, I thought again of Hélène's tears when, the previous year, she had told Papa that she was in love with a young immigrant, a man who had joined the Foreign Legion. I hoped that she and Jack would start a new life now far from Paris, in safety.

CHAPTER 8

PARIS UNDER OCCUPATION, SPRING-SUMMER 1941

PARIS BELONGED COMPLETELY to the occupying army now. Overnight we found ourselves living in a foreign city and a foreign nation. We were outsiders, pariahs, who feared every step we took and every word we might carelessly say could betray us to the enemy. German soldiers were in the streets, restaurants and shops; they were everywhere. They had the brazen air, easy laugh, and sneer of conquerors who owned the country. They wore dark gray uniforms, shiny black boots and gloves, and displayed their pistols prominently. Passersby stared at the soldiers in disbelief and horror; it had to be a bad dream that would surely dissolve in the morning light. Overnight restaurants displayed large signs on their doors: "No Admittance to Jews." One by one Jewish stores and businesses closed, and new owners put up signs with Aryan and German names.

It seemed like a lifetime ago when my brothers, sisters, and I rode the escalators of Monoprix as carefree children, staring at glittering merchandise that invited us to look, to touch, and to buy. Now the shelves of stores had few items for sale; everything of value was shipped off to Germany for German consumption, for the war. Long lines formed outside every grocery store and bakery. Once inside, you saw a few meager loaves of bread on almost bare shelves. Some items disappeared almost completely, like meat and butter. We were at first given ration cards, but these cards were not enough to feed our large family.

With each new anti-Jewish law enacted, Jews, and especially foreigners, became more and more aware of our status as "undesirables." By late spring of 1941, Jews were fired from businesses and professions such as teaching, banking, and editing. Many Jewish lawyers, doctors, pharmacists, dentists, and craftsmen lost their jobs. We began to see people rounded up and arrested by German or French policemen. Clusters of neighbors standing nearby on the street stopped to gawk at haggard men and women who were herded into trucks and suddenly whisked away. They were mostly immigrant families like ours. We overheard their Yiddish accents. We quickly learned to stay off the streets as much as possible and to not call attention to our accents. Daily survival was our new challenge.

Pétain made regular broadcasts on the radio. His once grandfatherly voice now had a sinister tone as we soon identified him with the Occupation. Gone was the French Republic with its Parliament and its protection of an individual's freedom. Now it was the "French State," just another name for German dictatorship. "Vichy" government meant Germany, even if the leaders pretended they were looking out for French interests. That's what Mama and Papa and my teachers told me. All laws protecting human rights were abolished. Almost every week Pétain signed new anti-Jewish laws that made it almost impossible for Jews to earn a living. Men and women stood in long lines outside welfare organizations to get food and clothing. The social service organizations were soon overwhelmed by their efforts to help everyone. I could see degradation and fear on the faces of all the Jews standing in line. Their eyes had the brooding, sunken look of hunted prey.

Papa could no longer work at the kosher store where he had been a ritual slaughterer. It all happened so unexpectedly, one warm late spring day in 1941 when I stopped by after school to meet him. Instead of being greeted by the friendly store owner who knew me by name and who used to ask me how school was going, I saw instead his young wife, now a widow, dressed completely in black, managing the store while her two small girls sat silently on the floor. Papa told me that the store owner had been killed by Germans—shot in reprisal for a German killed by a French Resistant. Papa told me to come home quickly with him. His face was ashen and he spoke in a deep, almost broken voice I could not recognize. He said he could no longer work there. His job had been eliminated. How could this be true? I wondered. Cruelty and violence made no sense at all to me. Maybe the store owner had been taken away to a labor camp or to a prison and he would return at the end of the war. Perhaps it had been a case of mistaken identity. I imagined that the store owner was still alive somewhere, hiding. Things were happening much too quickly for me to understand.

We continued to go to our synagogue on Saturday mornings. Since our temple was hidden in the courtyard of our apartment building and not visible from the street, it was a safer *shul* to attend, we thought. We soon discovered, to our horror, that we were mistaken. Papa was participating in a service one Saturday morning when suddenly a group of German soldiers burst into the building. One soldier demanded in his guttural French, "Who is the rabbi here?" "I am," Papa had answered calmly. The soldier smacked him across the face, knocking him backwards. "Don't you know that this is forbidden? *Juden*, get out!" Everyone rushed from the synagogue in a panic.

Papa retreated into his books to find consolation. He sat pensively in the dining room and his silences grew longer each day. Mama, on the other hand, grew more energized and defiant as the crisis deepened. She said our only hope for survival was for all of us to separate and to find shelter in the countryside. She told Bernard that he would have to find work on a farm, as would

Jacques. This would be Bernard's second attempt to leave Paris. Mama said that she would contact Hélène and her husband Jack in Nevers to ask them if they could look after me and my baby brother Max for a short time, until she found a permanent hiding place for us all. In the meantime, we would sell a few valuables on the black market and try to find some means of employment.

One day that June, the *concierge* of our building rushed out to warn our family that the police would soon be rounding up immigrants in our neighborhood. Rumors were circulating that some ethnic groups such as Romanians and Polish Jews were being targeted first. Mama sent Claire, Madeleine, Max, and me to spend the night in the apartment of an old French Jewish woman who lived in our building, Madame Klein. The old woman said she was sorry not to have candy or cookies to give us. Food had become so scarce. She gave us a few sugar cubes instead. We found that her soft, kindly voice soothed us and made us forget what was happening in the outside world for a few hours. She sighed heavily and said, "*C'est la guerre, mes enfants! Qu'est-ce qu'on peut faire?*" (It's war, my children. What can we do?)

Rosa, my school friend who had gone with me to Normandy just before the war, became my closest friend. Like my family, her parents were Polish immigrants and were poor. Rosa had an older sister and a younger brother who played the violin beautifully. When I visited her, I heard lovely violin music coming from the room where her brother was practicing, and sometimes at the same time, the whistling of a teapot on her kitchen stove. The two sounds were sweet and they harmonized in a strangely beautiful way. Sometimes she would visit me and we would meet inside, not daring anymore to play in the open courtyard. She said that her brother hoped to study to become a violinist one day when the war ended. That was my dream as well, I told Rosa. I could not talk about this subject now with Mama or Papa. With the

Nazis tightening their hold on France every day, I did not want to think about the future.

My sister Paulette came home one day with exciting news: she had just gotten engaged! Her fiancé, Maurice, like Jack and Hélène, was in the clothing business, so they would be able to continue working in Paris, at least for a while, without fears of deportation. Mama told me that the Germans gave an *Ausweis*, a protective document, to employees in industries considered essential to Germany. Paulette was only eighteen, yet I thought of her as my mature sister, almost like Mama. What would Paulette's wedding be like with our country occupied by the Germans? How would Paulette and Maurice stay safe? I didn't know what next week or next month had in store for us. Living through each day was becoming so difficult. I felt, though, that Mama would somehow find a way to hide us. Mama. . .

CHAPTER 9

DARK CLOUDS OVER PARIS,
JUNE-DECEMBER 1941

A STEADY HUM OF CONVERSATIONS reverberated through the crowded auditorium, with its long rows of wooden seats and elongated windows. Students from all the schools in our *arrondissement*—both private and public—came together on this day, June 12, 1941, for graduation. A cacophony of voices and laughter filled the large room, bouncing off its high ceiling. Small clusters of friends and classmates chatted excitedly here and there. Rosa and I sat together in one of the front rows, our heads leaning toward one another to share secrets. We spotted some of our teachers talking to people we did not recognize, who were probably teachers from other schools. Mademoiselle Rosenberg wore a slim gray suit with a small golden brooch on her collar. Mademoiselle Lazare wore a blue dress with padded shoulders. We noticed their fine shoes and stockings. Where would our friends and teachers go during the summer months, with German soldiers everywhere in Paris? In October, when high school classes were set to begin for us, would our teachers be able to return? It was a question we preferred not to dwell on, especially not that day and not at that moment.

"Mademoiselle Lew, Sora-Pesia." As my name was called, I walked to the front of the auditorium to receive the diploma from my principal, Monsieur Cohen, whose neatly trimmed mustache and slightly graying hair gave him a distinguished air.

The diploma, with its official stamp and lovely calligraphy, read: "Certificat d'Études Primaires" in large bold letters. In smaller bold letters I read my name, followed by my birth date and birthplace, "Dereczyn, Pologne." The other words blurred together as I felt my chest swelling with pride. I walked slowly back to my seat with my diploma.

I could see my dreams coming more clearly into focus: first of all, high school in the fall. When the war ended, I would take violin lessons. Violin music always brought tears to my eyes and I wanted to understand its magic. Someday I would play a violin well enough that others would feel the same powerful emotions that moved me. I knew that learning an instrument like the violin would be a long and difficult process, but I felt unexpectedly confident and believed I could be successful. I wanted to marry one day and have children of my own. I would try to be like Mama: brave, strong, and resourceful. I would share her love of theater, literature, and music.

Rosa woke me abruptly from my daydream. She had just received her diploma and wanted to show it to me. We congratulated each other and made plans to visit each other soon. I tried to hold back the tears running silently down my cheeks as we hugged and said goodbye. It was impossible to know what future awaited us both, but we knew better than to spoil graduation day by expressing those thoughts aloud.

In July, Pétain announced the "Aryanization" of all Jewish businesses and property. The money obtained from this liquidation of Jewish companies and property would go mainly to Germany, but Mama said that many French businesses would also enjoy a profit at the expense of the Jews, who were now destitute. She said that the anti-Jewish laws appealed to the greed of some French people and to their hatred of immigrants.

Lines of people waiting outside for food at welfare organizations grew longer each day. More and more Jews were unemployed and depended on these soup kitchens. It was shocking to see so many destitute people in the streets of Paris.

No one really knew what Pétain and the Germans were planning and what fate was in store for Jews in France. Some of our Jewish friends who were French seemed confident that their rights as citizens would be protected. Their families had lived in France for many generations and they identified themselves as French rather than as Jewish. We immigrants had no such feeling of security. There was no sure way of learning the truth about the war and our government's intentions, since the radio and newspapers were completely controlled by the Vichy government. As soon as you turned on the radio, you heard Nazi propaganda about Jews as parasites who were responsible for all of France's problems. Newspapers, all censored, were full of articles about Aryan businesses and about a future in which France would at last be free of greedy, arrogant Jews. Almost all Jewish newspapers stopped publishing as soon as the war began. A few illegal Jewish newspapers could still be obtained if you knew the right person to ask, but it was becoming more difficult to find one.

By summer, Papa no longer stepped outside the apartment. It was simply too dangerous. He buried himself in his prayer books and newspapers. He told us one day that, according to one Jewish newspaper, more than four thousand Jews had been arrested from the eleventh *arrondissement,* and taken to an internment camp in Drancy. Jewish welfare organizations were delivering food parcels to the inmates in Drancy and trying to assist the families of deported men. The inmates were mostly immigrants like us, but apparently some French Jews had also been arrested.

Mama went outside as infrequently as possible, just to buy a few groceries for us. She was afraid that a Christian neighbor might inform on her to the police, as soon as someone heard her Yiddish accent. The Vichy police offered monetary rewards to anyone who reported Jews to them, so neighbors had an incentive to become spies. Occasionally some Jewish neighbors were able to afford to buy a chicken on the black market. These neighbors would discreetly bring their chickens to Papa, who could then earn money as a *shohet* (ritual slaughterer). Mama earned a few extra pennies when those ladies asked her to clean the slaughtered chickens. Plucking chickens' feathers was hard, demanding, and dirty work. I did not like to see Mama working so hard. I felt upset about it, but I was smart enough to understand that those extra pennies would allow Mama to buy a chicken on the black market for our Sabbath dinner. Kosher food was now impossible to find in Paris.

Mama was very busy cleaning our apartment, cooking for nine of us, mending old clothes, and shopping for groceries. I helped Mama of course. She sometimes complained that I spent too much time folding clothes in the bedroom when she needed me in the kitchen. Shopping had become more and more difficult since the Germans depleted most stores. Mama waited in long lines to buy rationed foods such as eggs, milk, and cheese.

We depended more now on our *concierge* to warn us of imminent arrests in our building. Claire, Max, Madeleine, and I would spend the night with our neighbor, Madame Klein, whenever the *concierge* warned us about *rafles* (police roundups). Papa, Bernard, and Jacques hid in our attic when there were rumors of arrests. Mama was still searching for permanent hiding places for all of us: my older brothers would work on farms and the rest of us kids would go to two different towns. She reasoned that the more scattered we were throughout France, the better our chances of survival would be. Paulette and her fiancé Maurice were given an *Ausweis* (pass) that protected them from deportation, at least temporarily, since they worked in a clothing factory run by Germans. Jack, Hélène's husband, was well established in the provincial town of Nevers as the owner of a fabrics store, so he was not in immediate danger of deportation. Even though his store was officially closed, his customers knew him well and they came by discreetly to buy fabrics.

While French Jewish organizations seemed slow in responding to the national crisis, Jewish immigrant groups were starting to plan ways of fighting back. We read in a clandestine newspaper that one immigrant organization, M.O.I. (Immigrant Workforce), urged everyone to boycott products from German-run factories. This group was organizing a slowdown of production in factories and they were finding ways to sabotage machinery. The problem was that German-run factories were the only ones that allowed Jews to continue working without fear of being deported. Paulette and Maurice had to work in order to live, but all economic activity was helping Germany. Mama said it was impossible to solve this problem. Paulette and Hélène regularly gave Mama and Papa a small amount of money to help them make ends meet.

October brought us only more frightening news: the Nazis had bombed seven synagogues in Paris the previous week. I don't know how many people died in the fires. Our synagogue, fortunately, was not part of the central *Consistoire* (national Jewish organization) so it was not attacked. The secret Jewish communist organization, *Solidarité*, refused to allow Germans to have a propaganda victory. We read that they published an illegal pamphlet and managed to distribute it to about 25,000 people in Paris. In the leaflet, they warned Parisians about the campaign of racist propaganda and anti-Semitism that the pro-Nazi Vichy government was spreading and urged French people not to listen to their lies. According to Papa, new illegal newsletters had been sprouting every day, and some of them called for armed struggle against the occupiers. I heard that the newsletters warned about imminent roundups of Jews and wrote about conditions in the deportation camps to counter Nazi propaganda. Some even listed Protestant and Catholic institutions that were likely to hide Jews.

We heard rumors from neighbors that immigrant groups in Paris were starting to organize armed resistance against the Germans. The Germans were retaliating by executing hostages they selected at random, in an attempt to intimidate the entire French population. Jews were being singled out as hostages, even in "random" selections. My neighbor Madame Klein said that she saw a large poster displayed on a wall next to the grocery store that announced the execution of hostages. What a horrible world it had become!

When Rosa was not visiting me in my apartment, I tried to lose myself in books. For a few hours while I was reading, I could forget that war was just outside my window and that there was no end in sight to the killing. I could escape from my adopted country, a country that was now unrecognizable to me. Novels were my favorite type of books. The hero or heroine always lived in a world completely remote and distant and she or he always managed to overcome great obstacles. Russian novels were the best, I thought, but their sad endings always made me cry.

I don't remember how the summer disappeared, but I started my high school classes at long last. Viviane, my old friend from Place de la République, smiled but hardly spoke to me after class. She became more distant since she discovered boys. Her hair was styled and cut in a trendy way and her clothes looked chic. Perhaps we really had nothing in common since her family was wealthy and they did not feel as threatened by the Occupation.

November 30, 1941, I turned fifteen! Mama hugged me and Papa smiled happily. The rest of the family sang noisily, "Happy Birthday!" Mama prepared my favorite dish for me, potato *latkes*. Papa said that after the war we would celebrate birthdays in a bigger way. But then, we had to hope and pray for the future.

When I arrived at school one morning shortly after my birthday, I did not see any students milling about outside in the courtyard. As I opened the heavy front door, there was no hum of conversations in the hallway or nearby classrooms, only a strange, eerie silence. No lights had been turned on. I glanced down the dark hallway and thought I must have come to school on the wrong day. Could it have been Saturday? I started walking further and came to an empty classroom where a group of teachers were standing huddled together, their arms around each other's shoulders, sobbing quietly.

"School is closed, Sarah," one of my teachers said in a broken voice. "You should go back home. Monsieur Cohen, our principal, has been arrested. The Nazis took him away early this morning to an internment camp."

I froze, unable to move or to speak. It felt as though a door had just closed behind me, and in front of me I could see only darkness. The date was etched in my mind: December 12, 1941. Life would never again be the same.

CHAPTER 10

PARIS AND NEVERS, BURGUNDY, WINTER 1941–SPRING 1942

SCHOOL WAS CLOSED. My friends were scattered and in hiding. There was nothing to do but stay inside, read books, and help Mama with chores until my hiding place was ready. My childhood had ended abruptly but I was not yet a grown-up. I could feel the enemy's presence everywhere but did not see his face directly. I had to find ways of escaping and books became my biggest ally.

A few days later, on December 16, 1941, we learned the fate of my beloved principal, Monsieur Cohen, by reading a clandestine Jewish newspaper. On December 12, the Nazis had arrested 743 prominent Jewish intellectuals and civic leaders, including heads of companies, principals, professors, lawyers, doctors, engineers, and other notable French citizens. They were taken to an internment camp at Compiègne-Royalieu. Some were immediately deported to the east. On December 15, 1941, Monsieur Cohen and fifty-two other Jews were shot in retaliation for an attack against Germans by members of a Resistance group. Mama saw the following notice by General Stülpnagel posted in our neighborhood:

To strike those responsible for these cowardly attacks, I have ordered the following measures to be executed immediately:

1. a fine of one billion francs is imposed on all Jews of occupied France.

2. a large number of Jewish-Bolsheviks will be deported to forced labor in the East. . . Future deportations will be envisioned. . .

3. one hundred Jews, communists and anarchists. . . will be shot. These measures do not in any way affect French people, but only those individuals who are enemies of Germany, those who want to precipitate France's downfall, and whose goal it is to sabotage the reconciliation between Germany and France.

The Germans played their propaganda card shrewdly by displaying posters announcing executions and by exploiting the French press in order to isolate Jews. Jews were singled out as hostages and blamed for all of France's problems in the Vichy press, to turn public opinion against them and to distract the French from Nazi tyranny. The Germans were terrifying the entire country into submission. Even though Monsieur Cohen and the other fifty-two hostages who were shot were French citizens, the Germans claimed they were not French. "Real" French people wanted "reconciliation" with Germany, which we knew meant enslavement to the Nazi dictatorship.

We also read in the paper that *Solidarité*, the secret Jewish communist group, had organized strikes in two German-run factories, one manufacturing gloves and another men's knitwear. The strikes had just ended after several months. They had apparently succeeded in reducing production of goods sent to German soldiers and they had even sabotaged some machinery.

A new clandestine newsletter, *Cahiers du Témoignage Chrétien* (Notebooks of Christian Testimonial) appeared, published by a Jesuit priest named Father Chaillet. The headline in large bold letters read, "France, Watch Out! Don't Lose Your Soul!" It was good to know that some clergymen were at last protesting the persecution of Jews. We wondered, though, why we did not hear any voice of protest from the head of the Catholic Church in France.

February 1942 brought new anti-Jewish laws: Jews were forbidden to go outside between 8 pm and 6 am and had to surrender their bicycles and radios to the police station. Now our only source of information would be found in Jewish newspapers, and who knew how long they could continue running their secret presses before the police raided them? Life was becoming less bearable every day. Nazi roundups of Jews in Paris were proceeding on a larger scale than before. Paulette, on her way to work, saw large crowds of terrified people being herded into trucks guarded by French soldiers. It was a frightening development which we still could not believe, even after nearly two years of occupation: French soldiers were willingly carrying out the Nazis' orders in France. Would our *concierge* be able to warn us in time before the police raided our apartment building?

In May, a new law required all Jews over the age of six in the occupied zone to wear a yellow Star of David. It was to be displayed prominently on the left side of all outer garments. We had to comply with the law or face arrest. Mama sewed the star on my jacket. To me, it was just another humiliation that confirmed our status as outcasts. I wore mine for the first time as I walked to the grocery store in our neighborhood. Several people passed by without glancing at it. Then an elderly man caught a glimpse of my yellow emblem and said to me in a hushed voice, "Don't worry. We will take care of them." His quiet expression of support moved me. It made me realize that my French neighbors were not all hostile or indifferent to Jews.

Later that spring, Mama sent my little brother Max and me to hide with Hélène and Jack in Nevers, Burgundy until she could make financial arrangements with a Christian family for a more secure hiding place for us. Hélène and Jack now had a baby girl, Simone. Hélène was carrying the weight of the world on her shoulders. She and Jack secretly conducted business at their fabrics store, since the store was officially closed, so day-to-day survival was becoming a real challenge. Their baby needed nutritious foods which couldn't be found in stores. If the baby got sick, there was no medicine available and no doctor to consult since Hélène and Jack were hiding their Jewish identity. I could feel Hélène's distress without our exchanging a single word. It was better for Max and me to be outside as much as possible.

One day, Hélène told me to take Max for a walk in his stroller along the river bank. It was a mild, sunny morning with a hint of spring in the air. I followed a walkway next to the peaceful Loire River and Max made happy noises as he pointed to ducks in the river. After a while, I sat down on a bench and Max smiled contentedly next to me in his stroller. I told him to watch the ducks and I began to read a book I had brought along, a wonderful novel. The book transported me to a world where there was no German occupation and no roundup of Jews. The tranquility of the setting and the magic of fiction began to lull me. I felt at last relaxed and safe.

I looked up from the novel. The stroller was parked next to me but Max was gone. Had I lost my mind? My fascination with reading had destroyed all my common sense. "Max, Max!" I screamed. I ran and called Max's name everywhere. Panic overcame me and I sobbed uncontrollably. My baby brother Max was nowhere to be found and I was completely to blame. I would never forgive myself. Not only was there a river nearby where he might have drowned, but there were train tracks not far away. There was nothing I could do but run back to Hélène's home. "Max! Where are you?"

"Tu es folle, Sarah? Qu'est-ce que tu as fait? Ce n'est pas possible!" (Have you gone crazy, Sarah? What have you done? This is not possible!) Hélène stared at me, trembling. She and I had to go straight to the police station to report Max's disappearance, the police station where they might arrest Hélène and me and deport us. I was living my worst nightmare.

The middle-aged French police officer, of medium build, sat at his heavy oak desk when we walked into his office. He was smoking a cigarette and he rested it on his ashtray. His face looked surprisingly gentle as he glanced at the two of us. I did not dare speak. He recognized Hélène right away as Jack's wife. After listening to Hélène's frantic appeal for help, the French police officer smiled. "*Vous avez de la chance, vous savez. Un voisin a trouvé votre petit frère. Il est en sécurité chez une famille tout près d'ici.*" (You are very lucky, you know. A neighbor has found your little brother. He is staying safely with a family nearby.) As he smiled, the small creases around his eyes gave him the look of an uncle who was scolding us gently. Our words of gratitude could not express the debt we owed this officer, so different from many of his counterparts in Vichy France. We began to believe that the French police were not all cooperating with Nazi efforts to round up and deport Jews.

Apparently Max had wandered by himself to a nearby railroad crossing. He was bored since I hadn't been paying any attention to him. A neighbor had just taken a break from her knitting to look out her window. She and her husband lived on a hill overlooking the railroad crossing, and their job was to close a safety gate each time a train was approaching, to keep people, cars, trucks, and bicycles off the tracks. At the moment she looked out, she saw a small child wandering near the train tracks. She quickly ran out and grabbed him and brought him home. To her he was a little gift from heaven and she instantly fell in love with him. He had soft brown curly hair and almond-shaped dark eyes. Her husband, when he returned home, found his wife cuddling a little child and making playful noises to him. She explained everything to him and they discussed what to do. Couldn't they adopt him? She had always wanted a child. Her husband was a little more cautious. Shouldn't they inform the police first? That was the right thing to do. If afterwards no one claimed him, then they would be able to keep him.

My guilt was transformed into instant joy and relief. I would never tell my parents about what had happened, I decided. They were far away and didn't need to know about this. Not only was my beloved baby brother Max safe, a miracle in itself, but a French police officer had just protected us from deportation. He had known all along that we were Jewish and he had said nothing. Nevers was a town of miracles.

CHAPTER 11

HIDING IN NEVERS,
SPRING–SUMMER 1942

MAX AND I CONTINUED TO STAY at Hélène's home while she and Mama made arrangements for our next hiding place. Hélène had new woes: Jack had gone into hiding to avoid arrest. The Gestapo was hunting him down and he had left Nevers to find shelter in the "free zone." Jack had mailed a package of bread containing some money to his brother Daniel who was a prisoner in Germany, and the Nazis had opened his package. A French police officer had received orders from Germany to arrest Jack, but he had instead warned him of the upcoming police raid and had given him time to "disappear."

Hélène showed me a letter that Jack had mailed from his secret hiding place. It was addressed to their trusted Christian friends, the Thévenault family:

Very dear friends,

I send you my sincere wishes for your happiness. . . with the hope that we will soon see each other. If you only knew my ardent desire to see my wife again with my child. I cannot stop thinking about my child. I know that my wife is showering her with affection and that she does not miss me. It is I who miss her so terribly. I sent you a sealed letter, but in case it got lost, I am sending it again, and you will open it if something should happen to me. I don't believe in any of this, but you know that I am a man who thinks about every-

*thing. I dare to hope that we will see each other again soon in good
health, and that we will drink a bottle of fine wine together. . .*

See you soon.
Your friend,
Jack

Daily life was now a never-ending struggle for Hélène, who
was caring for their baby while continuing to work secretly at the
fabric store. Neighbors we thought we could trust might at any
moment inform on us to the police for a monetary reward. It was
best to stay indoors as much as possible and to avoid all conversations with strangers.

I was wearing my Star of David when I stepped outside and
began walking toward the center of town. I did not give much
thought to my badge until I noticed that neighbors passing by
on the street were stealing glances at my chest and giving me odd
looks. I began to walk more briskly to escape their glances.

Hélène had asked me to buy milk and cheese at a local dairy
store and when I arrived I stood in line outside the small store. I
decided that I would buy the items and walk back home quickly
before other neighbors could stare at me. My chest felt as if it were
burning with its blazing yellow emblem and I wanted to take off
my jacket. The line hardly moved at all, though. A group of teenagers stood in front of me in line. They were laughing and clown-
ing around with one another. One of them turned toward me,
saw my yellow star, and began to whisper to her friends. Another
friend pointed to my star and asked me with a snicker, "What is
that?" The three of them stepped away from me in disgust as if I
were contagious, all the while snickering. I ran away as fast as I
could, tears blinding me, and didn't stop running until I reached
Hélène's house. It didn't matter now that I had forgotten the milk
and cheese. Once inside I tore off my star and raced upstairs to
my bedroom. Hélène looked at me and soon understood what

had happened. We hugged each other and cried. I never wore the yellow star again.

New anti-Jewish laws were announced in July: Jews were denied access to all public places including the cinema, theater, parks, and beaches. We could shop only between three and four in the afternoon and we had to use the last car in the Métro and the last row of seats in buses. Jewish newspapers reported that some Christians were wearing a yellow Star of David badge out of solidarity, a hopeful sign that Nazi propaganda was beginning to backfire. Even if some French people were anti-Semitic, we knew that they hated the occupiers even more. French people as a whole did not want to cooperate with the Nazis. Though some were profiting from the liquidation of Jewish businesses and property, we learned that many more found ways to assist Jews.

The Resistance organization *Solidarité* had begun its armed struggle against the Germans in France but they were suffering very heavy losses. For each German killed, the Nazis executed hundreds of hostages. According to clandestine newsletters, over 900 hostages had already been murdered in Paris. It was a terrible cycle of attacks and reprisals that Hitler hoped would crush all resistance.

Hélène asked some trusted Christian friends near Nevers to hide Max and me for a few weeks. Monsieur and Madame Leclair were old friends of Jack and Hélène. They knew one another through Jack's business. In his conversations with Hélène, Monsieur Leclair had said that we were all in a struggle against the German aggressors. It did not seem to matter to them that we were Jewish. For the Leclair family, Jack and Hélène were French, just as they themselves were. Madame Leclair was a heavy-set, middle-aged woman and Monsieur Leclair was a gray-haired, quiet man whose eyes had a gentle twinkle. When we arrived, they greeted us warmly and showed Max and me to our bedroom upstairs. Their whitewashed house had cheerful curtains and dark polished furniture.

The weeks we spent at their home flew by fast. Madame Leclair fed us very well, and Max and I, as hungry, growing children, loved the dishes she prepared. Monsieur Leclair would read the newspaper every evening and would sigh, "*Qu'est-ce que notre pauvre pays va devenir?*" (What will become of our poor country?) After dinner, I helped Madame Leclair clear the table and wash dishes. The gentle couple helped me to forget my humiliation at the dairy store. When we parted, our hugs and words of thanks could not express what was on my mind: that these strangers had risked their own lives to hide us.

In July, Max and I were back home in Paris. My brothers and sisters still did not have their hiding places in the countryside, so we all depended on our *concierge* to warn us of police raids. Bernard, Jacques, Max, and Papa would hide in the attic, and my sisters and I would hide at Madame Klein's apartment. Mama did not believe that the French police would arrest women or children. She felt more worried about Bernard and Jacques, teenage boys, whom the Nazis might send to forced labor camps. Paulette and Mama were making contacts with Christian families in Rogny-les-Sept-Écluses (Burgundy) and Le Guédeniau (Maine-et-Loire) to hide us all, once the financial arrangements were completed.

My life in Paris resumed its monotonous routine. I stayed inside the apartment almost every day. I helped Mama with household chores and read my novels whenever I had a free moment. I found most of these novels nearby in an old library that smelled of mold and dust. I think I was the only patron to frequent this small library since the war had begun. Papa was quiet and withdrawn as ever. He sat engrossed in his prayer books in the dining room, searching for solace. We had become accustomed to his silence. Claire and I liked to talk about school memories, our old friends and teachers. We wondered where they all were today, if they were safe, and when the war would finally end.

One night, when Claire and I were sleeping soundly in our shared bed, there was a sudden loud knock on the front door. We both sat up in bed, startled and trembling. Then we heard Mama's voice speaking to some men. I heard a clamor of footsteps running up to the attic. It must have been Papa, Max, Bernard and Jacques. We pushed our goose blanket off the bed and heard Mama's voice again, speaking calmly. Claire and I huddled together. We could hear two French police officers asking her for identification. *"Certainement, Messieurs. Je vais la trouver tout de suite. Vous aimeriez un peu de thé?"* (Certainly, *Messieurs*. I'll get it for you right now. Would you like some tea?) I whispered to Claire, "Why is Mama offering tea to the policemen? They came to arrest us!" *"Merci, Madame. Bonne nuit."* (Thank you, *Madame*. Good night.) I heard our front door close and footsteps fade away down the stairs. Mama came into our bedroom to reassure us. "They were very polite. Fortunately, Paulette's pass protected us once more. It's all right now, children. Go back to sleep." I thought to myself after she left the room: would Paulette's pass be enough to save us the next time?

CHAPTER 12

ARRESTS IN PARIS, SUMMER 1942

JULY 1942 WAS OPPRESSIVELY HOT. Unremitting waves of sunlight bore down on Paris and left its war-weary inhabitants listless and subdued. Passersby on the street slowed their pace to a crawl and a few mangy dogs slumped in doorways. Mama came home wilted from her errands and sat down next to Papa. "Our neighbor Madame Relman found a leaflet from *Solidarité* warning about an upcoming *rafle* (police roundup). You must all go over to Madame Klein's apartment. You will be safe in her attic. The French police are not going to arrest women, so I am not concerned about my own safety. Paulette and I will stay here."

There was more disturbing news in the Jewish newspapers. Allied troops were battling German forces in North Africa, Russia and even in the Pacific, with heavy Allied losses. The European continent and most of the world were engulfed now in war, a never-ending war. Some Christian friends stayed away from us and our Jewish friends struggled to find hiding places. My closest friend, Rosa, who had hid in an attic the previous week with her sister, told me that her parents and brother had been arrested by the French police. She was too overcome with grief to say any more. It was hard for us to accept the silence of most of the French nation to our fate. Mama said she couldn't understand why more clergymen and ordinary men and women didn't listen to their own conscience and speak out against so much evil in France.

According to Jewish newspaper reports, Pétain and his corrupt cohorts were letting French policemen carry out massive arrests of Jews in the occupied zone. The illusion that persecutions were imposed on France by Germany was now shattered. We knew that Pétain had signed all the anti-Jewish laws that made us easy targets for arrest.

The knock on our front door came just before dawn on July 16. Paulette and Mama were alone this time in the apartment, while the rest of us were hiding in Madame Klein's attic. Paulette showed her pass to two French officers, who told her that it was no longer valid. They had orders to arrest all foreign Jews in Paris, including women and children. Paulette and Mama were taken away by bus.

The next few days passed in a fog. Where were Mama and Paulette? How were they surviving? Would we ever see them again? We had no answers and no one could ease my anxiety. Papa seemed to age overnight; his face had a grayish hue. We sat around silently in the apartment, barely able to eat or drink. Three days later, Paulette came back home at last, her face ashen. But where was Mama? It was difficult for her to tell us what had happened. Her voice began to break and her hands shook as she tried to speak.

"They took us to the Vélodrome d'Hiver, a cycling arena in the fifteenth *arrondissement.* There were thousands of us crammed together in the stifling heat, with no food or water. All of us were terrified. Children separated from their parents were crying hysterically. Old men and women began to faint from the heat. The French police were standing guard. Their faces showed no human emotion. They just stared straight ahead like automatons. I could not recognize them as Frenchmen. They surrounded us, their rifles aimed at anyone who tried to escape.

"I showed an officer my *Ausweis* (pass) and told him he had no right to hold my mother and me there. He agreed finally to release me but said there was no guarantee that my mother would be protected from deportation by my pass. He told me they were taking her to Drancy tomorrow."

Days passed. We remained in the dark, afraid to think about the future. Paulette went to Drancy every day to demand the release of Mama, risking her own life as she faced the police. Claire and I huddled together in our bed at night and slept fitfully when exhaustion finally overcame us. Paulette, now taking on the role of mother, became braver and more defiant as the days passed. She confronted the French authorities relentlessly.

The Jewish newspapers confirmed our worst fears: an army of nine thousand French policemen, on July 16–17, had arrested more than 13,000 Jews in Paris, along with Mama and Paulette. The *Rafle du Vel d'Hiv,* as it was now called, had shown beyond any doubt that the Vichy government was working with Hitler to murder the Jewish population of France. For the first time in France even women and children were arrested. Men and women, sick and old people were locked up together without water in the blazing heat. The newspaper article said that out of thirteen thousand victims, ten thousand were women and children. The writer thought that many men must have hidden without their families because no one believed that the French police would be so inhuman as to arrest young children and women.

Paulette came home the next day in tears. She told us between sobs that she had at last convinced a police officer to release Mama and that after the police had inspected her clothing, they found in her pocket some hidden letters from other inmates. "You know how good-hearted Mama is. She could not leave other women alone in Drancy when they begged her to give messages to their families. The police officer locked her up again in camp for breaking the rules."

We continued to wait, day after day, for news about Mama as Paulette went to Drancy to plead for her release. We knew that she might be deported to the East, but we didn't dare to speak about this possibility to each other. Instead, Papa kept the youngest kids, Max and Madeleine, busy by teaching them history from the Scriptures.

News of the *Vel'd'Hiv* roundup spread quickly and Vichy authorities were unable to prevent protest letters from circulating throughout France. The arrests had touched a nerve and Christians who had long been silent were finally making their voices heard. Papa read in the newspaper that several prominent clergymen, including Cardinal Suhard, Pastor Boegner, and Archbishop Saliège had sent letters to Pétain, demanding that he put an end to the persecution of Jews. Cardinal Gerlier, head of the French Catholic Church, rescued eighty-four Jewish children from the police, after they had been arrested in Lyon. The organization "Christian Friendship" rescued thousands of Jews in Lyon who were about to be deported. Clandestine Christian newspapers and French radio broadcasts from London were stirring up public outcry at the plight of the Jews. But would Mama be released?

Claire and I talked constantly about how our life had changed. We thought of our long train trip from Dereczyn to Paris almost six years before and our hope that Paris would be a city where we could start a new life. Nothing had turned out the way we had planned. The future was terrifying to think about. One night, before sleep overtook me, I thought of Rosa, whose family had been deported. I could hear her young brother playing his violin in their apartment. I pictured his violin lying in its case in an empty apartment, its music silenced. Where was her family now? I wondered.

PHOTO GALLERY

Sarah's parents, Rabbi Avraham Moshe Lew and
Sheina Michlah Gorinowski, at the time of their
engagement, in 1918, in Dereczyn, Poland.

Sarah's father, Rabbi Avraham Moshe Lew.
Paris, in early 1937.

Sarah's mother and siblings in early 1937. Top row, from the left: Paulette, Mother, Helene; middle row: Jacques on left, Bernard on right; bottom row, from the left: Claire, Madeleine, and Sarah.

A school trip to Normandy in August, 1939. Sarah's principal, seated in the center, in front of a mirror, was killed by the Nazis in December, 1941.

Sarah's younger brother Max Lew. Paris, in early 1940.

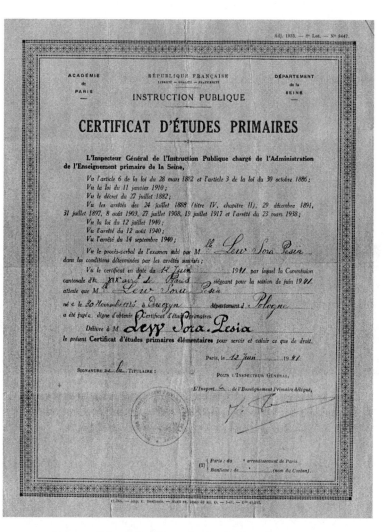

Primary School Certificate for Sarah (Sora Pesia Lew),
dated June 12, 1941, Paris.

Sarah in Nevers, Burgundy, in early 1942. Sarah is seated in the center, holding her baby niece, Simone. Her sister and brother-in-law, Hélène and Jack, are seated at a table on the right.

Sarah in May, 1944, upon
her arrival in Switzerland.
Sarah is 17 years old.

Sarah's nursing school class. Early 1945, in Territet, Switzerland.
Sarah is at the top left.

Wir bestätigen, dass
Nous certifions que

Melle. Sarah L E W

geboren am   in Deruzyl, Polen
né(e) le 30. 11. 1926   à

einen Kurs absolviert hat für
a suivi un cours de

Puériculture

im Flüchtlingsheim / Arbeitslager
au home pour réfugiés / camp de travail

Mont-Choisi, La Rosiaz s/Lausanne

in der Zeit vom   bis
du 15 novembre 1944   au 15 mars 1945

Die Schlussprüfung wurde abgelegt mit
L'élève a subi l'examen final avec

Mention: B i e n

Kurs und Prüfung umfassten nachstehende Fächer
Le cours et l'examen comportaient les branches suivantes

Theorie
théorie   Anatomie
          Puériculture
          Alimentation du Nourrisson

Praktische Arbeit
travail pratique
          Soins au Nourrisson
          Diététique

Die Fachexperten   Die Heimleitung
pour les experts   la direction du home/camp

Département fédéral de
Justice et Police
Division de Police
Home pour réfugiés „Mont Choisi"
LA ROSIAZ-Lausanne

ZENTRALLEITUNG DER ARBEITSLAGER
DIRECTION CENTRALE DES CAMPS DE TRAVAIL

Der Chef - le chef

Otto Zaugg

Zürich, den 1 April 1945.
Zurich, le

Sarah's Nursing School Certificate. "Sarah Lew has satisfactorily
completed a course in infant care, November 15, 1944 to
March 15, 1945; Lausanne, Switzerland."

CHAPTER 13

HIDING IN LE GUÉDENIAU, SUMMER 1942

MAMA WAS RELEASED FROM DRANCY at last. She came back home to our apartment thin and very pale, but her long ordeal had not broken her spirit. My pain changed to instant joy as we hugged and cried. Paulette had taken her life in her hands each day over the past several weeks when she had gone to Drancy to plead for her release. She had at last convinced the police that her *Ausweis* was valid and that they had no right to detain Mama. Paulette said that she had witnessed a cattle car filled with Jews being deported from Drancy.

What Mama and Paulette had witnessed in Drancy haunted them. "I will never forget the sight of children, some as young as two or three years old, separated from their mothers, terrified and hungry. I can still hear their wailing day and night," Mama said. "The rest of us women tried to care for the little ones. We washed them and gave them any food we had. We told them that their parents would be back before long. There was terrible sanitation at the camp, only a few toilets for thousands of people. Even so, many young women managed to wash themselves with the meager water supply available. The French guards did nothing at all to help and gave us no food for days."

We knew the French police would be back to raid our apartment and to arrest us. It was time to put Mama's plan into action immediately. With help from Paulette, Mama had found hiding places for all of us. We had managed to buy forged identification cards and ration coupons on the black market. Madeleine and I were going to the village of Le Guédeniau in Maine-et-Loire, while Max and Claire would be sent to the village of Rogny-les-Sept-Écluses, in Burgundy. Both Bernard and Jacques had found shelter on farms. Mama and Papa would move to a secret apartment that Paulette had obtained for them at 25 Rue Lancry, near Place de la République. They would share an apartment with another Jewish couple who had a teenage son. Paulette would remain in Paris, protected by her *Ausweis*, since she and her fiancé were able to work at their German-run clothing factory.

Almost all of our Jewish neighbors who had not already left Paris were searching for shelter in the countryside. Since Jews had lost their means of employment after Pétain passed his anti-Jewish laws, they often did not have the resources to escape to villages in the south. Hélène and Paulette's income helped to pay for our lodging. Those Christian families who agreed to help us were risking their own lives, since their neighbors could have them deported. I repeated to myself once more the instructions Papa and Mama had given me: "Your name is 'Suzanne' and you are Catholic. Eat the food they serve you even though it is not kosher, help around the house, and don't talk to strangers in the village. Don't make yourself stand out in any way." I remembered the tiny piece of paper, now tucked away in my shoe for safekeeping, with Mama and Papa's new French names and their secret Paris address.

Le Guédeniau, a small village in the Loire valley, was a two-hour train journey from Paris. Through our train window we gazed at wheat fields and countless towns with their medieval churches, reminders of centuries past that might have enchanted us if we hadn't been so lonely and homesick already. The village itself was surrounded by acres of forests, farm land and orchards. An old stone watermill turned its heavy wheel on the Brocard River.

Madame Monbrun greeted Madeleine and me at her doorway. Madeleine held my arm more tightly as we stepped into her drab living room. We were both frightened and worn out after our dangerous train ride, the first trip we had made on our own outside of Paris. Madame Monbrun was an old woman with deep lines on her forehead and wispy gray hair. She wore a shapeless patterned dress that hung loosely from her shoulders. The interior of her house was dimly lit and airless, despite several windows. The furniture, stained dark, was covered with worn, dirty upholstery. I wished right then that I could turn around and take a train back to Paris.

Madame Monbrun quietly showed us our bedroom and gave us a quick tour of the house. I tried to listen to Madame Monbrun's instructions about where to put my clothes and what chores I would do in the kitchen. I heard them but my mind kept racing back to Paris and to my family. I didn't see how I would be able to live for months or years with this stranger in her gloomy house. Madeleine looked as miserable as I felt.

Our errands for Madame Monbrun brought us each day to the village center. Le Guédeniau consisted of a main street leading to the heart of the village—a town square bordered by lime trees. On the square stood the *Mairie* (city hall), a few small shops, and further down the street, a twelfth-century stone church. The main street ended in a semi-circle, where we were drawn to the sound of hammering emanating from an old blacksmith shop. Madeleine and I often watched with fascination as the blacksmith heated and pounded the iron with great skill to produce horseshoes for the local farmers' horses. The only café in the village served many functions: it was at once a restaurant, a café, and a shop. At this end of Main Street, another small street branched off, where I could see neat white limestone homes and cottages, each surrounded by a small garden.

On our walk back from the village center the next day, we passed a neighbor standing in her front yard who smiled at us and invited us both inside.

"Are you relatives of Madame Monbrun?"

"No, we're friends visiting from Paris," I said, trying to answer as we had been told. I told her something about my parents' friendship with Madame Monbrun and said that we enjoyed visiting the countryside. Our neighbor sighed in agreement. "*Paris, c'est tellement triste aujourd'hui. La guerre, c'est interminable.*" (How sad it is in Paris today. The war is never-ending). She served us cold drinks and biscuits and admired Madeleine's braids.

Her friendly curiosity warmed me, made me forget the war and our loneliness. I even began to forget about Mama's warnings. Our neighbor told us about the market every Saturday and about church gatherings on Sundays. "Which church do you usually go to?" Without even thinking I blurted out, "We're Jewish. We don't go to church." Lying was just not in my nature. She looked startled. "*Mais non, ce n'est pas possible. Vous n'êtes pas juives. Les Juifs ont des cornes.*" (No, that's not possible. You can't be Jewish. All Jews have horns.) We quickly took leave of our neighbor. I worried that my naïveté might have jeopardized our safety. I also felt ashamed that I had forgotten all of Mama's warnings so easily. What if this neighbor were to contact the Vichy police?

Madeleine and I ate our meals mostly in silence with Madame Monbrun and then we helped her tidy up the kitchen. The dishes she served left us hungry. We could not adjust to her vegetable stews and dry bread, the same bland and tasteless dishes she prepared every day. We learned about her life in the old days, when her husband had been alive. "*Mon pauvre mari*" (my poor husband), she would reminisce. Then she would sigh, "*C'était le bon vieux temps*" (Those were the good old days).

I walked by an empty bedroom next to ours. It had a narrow bed, a small oak desk and a chair covered with a frayed cloth. The old lady caught my gaze and lowered her eyes as she spoke with a pained expression. "That room belongs to Jean, my son." She paused for a moment before continuing. "He's in an institution a long distance away. He lost his sight as a young child. I can only afford to visit him very rarely. I told you that my husband passed away two years ago. *La vie, c'est dure, mes enfants.*" (Life is hard, my children.)

We could not get accustomed to the dust that lay on every piece of furniture, even after I thought we had tidied up, nor to the insects and mice that scurried around. We found the village strangely still, both day and night, and nothing happened to distinguish one day from the next. I felt constantly homesick. I missed Paris, my family, my old life. On top of this, my scalp began to itch unexpectedly and it kept me tossing and turning at night. I touched my scalp and found lice crawling on my hand. I decided not to mention it to Madame Monbrun. It was something I felt ashamed and embarrassed about. Perhaps it would go away if I washed my hair with more soap and scrubbed harder.

We wrote to Mama and Papa every few weeks at their secret address and waited anxiously for Mama's letters to arrive. We had to buy stamps at a nearby town. Stamps were costly and sending letters was a little risky, so we learned to be prudent. The highlight of our days was when we saw the postman walking down the dirt path toward our house. On some days there would be an envelope with Mama's familiar handwriting on it. She could always read our thoughts between the lines of our letters. She told us to be patient and brave. We were safe in Le Guédeniau. There were no German soldiers there and no French *Milice* (Vichy police force). Wasn't that the most important thing right now, to be safe from deportation? If we were all patient, we would be together again before long when the war ended.

Madame Monbrun began to complain to us that her monthly payments had stopped coming. I knew that living in Paris was becoming harder each day for Mama and Papa. Stores had barely a few loaves of bread left on their shelves, since all goods were shipped to Germany or given to the occupying army in France. Mama had to purchase food on the black market at exorbitant prices.

One day Madame Monbrun said that she would not be able to keep us any longer at her house. But I could not become a burden on my parents. I knew I had to find some employment in Le Guédeniau and a new shelter for Madeleine and myself. I was fifteen years old and Madeleine was eight. The two of us were on our own now.

CHAPTER 14

WAITING,
AUTUMN, 1942–SUMMER 1943

WHERE WOULD MADELEINE and I go, now that Madame Monbrun was sending us away? I wondered. I decided to ask for a job at the café in the village. But what about Madeleine, who was not yet nine years old? I couldn't support her on my own. She was lonely, miserable, and homesick in Le Guédeniau. I didn't want to give Mama and Papa an extra burden. They were already struggling in Paris with serious food shortages and with the daily risk of being betrayed by their neighbors.

It was early autumn and the Indian summer days were unseasonably hot. My isolation made it seem as though I had been living in Le Guédeniau for years. The Nazis were tightening their grip on France and the Vichy government ordered the French *Milice* in all regions of France to arrest Jews. Reports of the shocking *Vélodrome d'Hiver* roundup had fueled our fears that even children were not safe from deportation. We knew that Jews were being sent in cattle cars to camps in Poland and Germany, where conditions were more than terrible.

Mama contacted Monsieur and Madame Ducerf, a young Catholic couple in Nevers, where Claire and Max were staying. They agreed to take Madeleine as a boarder, as long as Claire, fourteen years old, would pick her up at Mama and Papa's hiding place near Place de la République in Paris and bring her to their home. It would be dangerous for a child as young as Madeleine to travel alone on a train to Paris, especially since the *Milice* were everywhere, checking identification cards. But there was no other choice.

Madeleine and I went over instructions again for the trip. "If a police officer stops you, you must show him your forged identification card. Never reveal that you are Jewish or where your parents live. Do not speak to anyone during the train ride. Memorize Mama and Papa's address, in case you lose the paper I gave you." I didn't dare say my thoughts aloud: if I had been unable to lie about my own identity to a stranger in Le Guédeniau, how could Madeleine, not yet nine years old, be expected to? She looked up at me anxiously. The Occupation made no sense to her. "Why are we always hiding? Why do they hate us here?" I had no answers to her questions.

Madeleine stood next to me, tears welling up in her dark eyes, as the train pulled into the station. I told her that we would all be together again soon. She would see Mama and Papa later that day in Paris. "Do you remember their address?" I asked. "Yes, I think so," she said, tentatively. She checked the small piece of paper carefully hidden in her pocket. "You must never tell it to anyone you meet. Will you remember that?" I said. "Yes," she said, in a very small voice.

She slowly climbed onto the train, carrying a basket on her arm with a live chicken in it. She looked back at me nervously. It was my idea to surprise Mama and Papa with the chicken. She was bringing it home so that they would have their first kosher meal in many months. Since they had gone into hiding, it had been impossible to obtain kosher food. Madeleine looked even younger than her years as she stared out the train window, slowly waving goodbye.

I went immediately to the café in the village and asked a young woman standing at the counter if they needed a maid. Her husband came out from the back room to meet me. He looked at me with a probing stare as he checked my forged identification card. "Yes, we do, but I'm afraid we can't offer you much salary. *C'est la guerre, vous savez, c'est difficile.*" (It's wartime. Times are hard, as you know.) "Furthermore, you cannot stay here at night. It is too dangerous for us to let you live here. We will find you another building where you can sleep." They had caught my slight foreign accent and had sized up my refugee demeanor. They could not risk their lives for a Jewish girl like me. I acquiesced and put on the oversized apron they handed me, which made my thin frame seem even more frail.

A letter arrived from Claire one week later. Claire, normally not a long-winded letter writer, had written four long pages in her careful handwriting. I had to sit down to devour the whole story of Madeleine's trip. Madeleine had arrived safely in Paris. Fortunately no police officers had stopped her *en route*.

> *. . . Madeleine told us that she was frightened when she exited from the Métro in Paris and went searching for Mama's apartment building. She wandered from building to building, looking for an address and afraid to ask anyone for help. She looked down frequently on her little piece of paper and up again at each building. Then she saw a café that looked familiar. Finally, she knocked on one door and waited an eternity for someone to answer. It was Mama!*

Claire's letter continued on the next page:

> *After many hugs and some rushed conversation, Madeleine and I set out again by train for Burgundy. There was no time to enjoy a kosher meal made from her chicken. We needed to arrive by nightfall since Mama and Papa's apartment had no space for us to spend the night. We had to change trains in order to reach the small town of Rogny-les-Sept-Écluses. The two of us stood on a train platform in the broiling sun for what seemed like forever. No train arrived. A young woman who had seen us both earlier on the train walked by and noticed our forlorn expression. She asked us where we were*

going and was stunned to learn of our destination. 'Mais il n'y a plus de trains aujourd'hui pour Rogny-les-Sept-Écluses.' (There are no more trains today for Rogny-les-Sept-Écluses.) 'What are you going to do?' She looked pensive. 'Let me think a little.'

She had an idea. 'There is another train you could take that stops here in an hour or so. It will take you to a nearby town and then you can walk the rest of the distance. The town is about ten miles from Rogny-les-Sept-Écluses,' she said. The kindly lady invited us to her home nearby for a cool drink. She put a little extra money in Madeleine's pocket for the long trip and wished us both well as we left for the station.

After arriving at the 'nearby' town, Madeleine and I walked in the heat along a treeless country road. I carried Madeleine's bundle of clothes along with my own. Some peasants passed by us on the road. They were riding in mule-drawn wagons. None offered to give us a ride. We walked for more than three hours and did not reach Madame Ducerf's home until long after nightfall. Both of us collapsed from thirst and exhaustion at their home. What a trip!

I folded up Claire's letter. Claire and Madeleine had arrived safely in Burgundy, a miracle in itself. Their chance encounter with a stranger had helped them and now Monsieur and Madame Ducerf would keep them safe and alive. The Ducerf family risked being denounced by their neighbors to the police, yet they had agreed to hide three children from our family. They hated the Pétain government almost as much as we did and their kindness was also an act of defiance and patriotism. I was moved by their compassion. Would our non-Jewish neighbors in Dereczyn have risked their lives to help us? I doubted it.

I gradually settled into my new routine. During the day, I cleaned the kitchen for my new employers, Monsieur and Madame Leroy. They were demanding and glad to exploit me, since they knew I had no choice but to stay. There were dishes to wash, floors to clean, and of course sweeping to do in the kitchen. I stood for most of the day. Later in the evening I was given a meal that was much better than Madame Monbrun's dishes. Madame Leroy would sometimes let me hold her baby. The hardest part for me was the constant itching of my scalp, which no amount of washing could alleviate. I avoided touching my head as long as I could, but at times I could not bear it any longer. When I saw myself reflected in the mirror on the back wall of the café, I was hard to recognize. I was sixteen, but my face already had a grown-up woman's pallor, probably because of loneliness and poor nutrition. I had lost my girlish look and my sunny disposition. My figure had become womanly and I could feel the glances of teenage boys in the café and in the streets outside. On Sundays as I walked through the village center, some boys would begin to follow me and tease me. "*Regarde la belle. Tu as un petit ami?*" (Look at the pretty girl. Do you have a boyfriend?) They continued to walk behind me and I did my best to ignore their remarks. I worried that they might follow me at night when I walked home alone.

I would leave work at 9 or 10 p.m. each evening. My new "home" was an abandoned building on the outskirts of town, where I occupied an empty room on the first floor with no running water, toilet, or electricity. Above me, an eccentric old man lived by himself. I worried about him coming into my room at night. To reach the dilapidated building, I had to find my way across the village at night with no streetlights. Sometimes I stumbled in the dark and scraped my legs against sharp bushes. When I could not find my way back to the main street I would sob quietly to myself. As my eyes adjusted to the dark, I could make out the flickering of tiny fireflies that lit up bushes along the road. They became a comforting sight, my new silent companions in the darkness.

Even though I was exhausted from working all day, I would not go to sleep right away. I washed as best as I could with a bucket of cold water and spent a lot of time combing my hair, trying without success to get rid of the lice. On the floor in my room, I could hear the scratching noises of rats as they scurried around. It always sent shivers down my spine. I imagined them coming into my bed and running all over me. As I lay down, I pulled a blanket over my head to keep them out. Then my scalp would itch and I would rub it. During the night, I thought about my family so far away and wished I could see them. The daylight was a welcome relief.

Next to my dilapidated house was a convent where I sometimes noticed nuns coming and going. One nun stopped me during my walk into the village and invited me to church on Sunday. I managed to give an evasive answer. After this first encounter I tried hard to avoid meeting other nuns. I often passed the Le Guédeniau church but never stepped inside.

As I walked through the village early each morning, I caught a glimpse of a small lake, and beyond it a lovely château surrounded by a high stone wall, visible on a hilltop. Carefully tended gardens covered the hills around the château. I tried to imagine the aristocratic family that lived there. Did they have a teenage daughter about my age? Did they enjoy fine food in an elegant dining room, dining together in luxury? Then I escaped from my dreary routine for a short time and appreciated the beauty of Le Guédeniau.

One day, Monsieur Leroy told me that the Germans had surrendered in Stalingrad. The Allies were winning in North Africa as well. There was hope that the war would end. In France, however, the Germans now occupied the entire country and there was no longer a "free zone." Deportations of Jews and Resistants were proceeding at a very fast pace even in the south of France.

In the early summer, we heard terrible news from Hélène: Jack had been arrested. He had heeded the French police officer's warning to go into hiding and had been staying for many months just south of Nevers. One day, however, he had crept back into his home to see Hélène and his baby daughter Simone once more.

It was hard for him to be away from them for long and to know that his family would be alone, without any protection against the Nazis. But his visit came at a great cost: the Nazis were waiting for him outside when he arrived.

And, during that summer of 1943, I became ill.

CHAPTER 15

A VISIT WITH JACQUES, SUMMER 1943

THE ALLIES WERE WINNING in North Africa and in the North Atlantic as well, where forty-one German U-boats had just been sunk. But in France, the war dragged on without a glimmer of hope for victory. The collaborationist chief of police, René Bousquet, organized a massive police roundup of Jews in Marseille and deported two thousand people. French gendarmes were arresting women, men, and children at alarming rates in towns and cities throughout France. No region of France was safe. I did not witness any arrests in Le Guédeniau, but I could never breathe freely knowing that Mama and Papa, along with the rest of the family, faced dangers every day.

One day followed another without end. I did chores each morning, afternoon, and evening in the village café. Then I walked in the darkness back to my depressing "home." There was no distinction between weekend or weekday, between winter or spring, except for an extra sweater I wore on cold days. At least during the day I kept busy sweeping and cleaning, so that my mind could wander freely back to Paris, where Rosa, Mama and Papa, and Paulette were hiding. I thought about what they might be doing and I sometimes remembered a phrase Mama or Rosa had said that made me smile. I also thought about school and about my teacher, Mademoiselle Lazare, who had praised my compositions.

The highlight of my day was now an occasional friendly "hello" from neighbors as I walked through the village each morning.

On one such morning, a young couple sitting on their front porch motioned for me to come over to chat. They invited me into their well-kept, neatly decorated home. I learned that they were both teachers who had moved there recently from another town. They asked me some questions but did not push me to reveal a lot about myself. A certain distance between us led me to believe that they had secrets they did not wish to disclose and they suspected that I did as well. Perhaps they too were Jews hiding in Le Guédeniau. It was enough for me to know that I had some friendly neighbors whom I could talk to, when loneliness weighed me down.

One Sunday, on this same street, an old woman who was gardening stopped to watch me pass by her home. She came over to me and invited me inside for tea. She looked at me kindly as we walked together into the kitchen of her clean, limestone house. She must have noticed that I was rubbing my scalp. "*Mademoiselle*, I think I can cure your problem." After carefully trimming my brown hair with her scissors, she began to pour a strange-smelling liquid over my scalp and to massage it into my roots. "This is benzene, *Mademoiselle*." She bent over me and finally washed out the benzene after several minutes. I stood up to thank her and smiled for the first time in many months. There was no longer an itching sensation in my scalp. I did not know how to repay this gentle woman, a complete stranger who had saved me from the torture of those horrible lice.

With one health problem solved, a new one appeared unexpectedly. My menstrual period stopped coming and I began to look unwell. As I caught my reflection in the café mirror, I was startled to see the transformation. My face had become somewhat swollen and my arms and legs looked bloated. I did not like what I saw. Eating by myself, feeling lonely and getting little fresh air and rest were affecting my health. Of course, it was out of the question to speak to a doctor in Le Guédeniau.

I decided instead, one Sunday, to visit my older brother Jacques, the only family member who lived within walking distance from Le Guédeniau. I had found a job for him at a nearby farm. The main road out of Le Guédeniau was lined with poplar trees. It was a mild summer morning and the towering poplars swayed gracefully in the breeze. The bucolic scene made me forget momentarily that Germans might be lurking in farmhouses nearby. I double-checked the forged identification paper tucked in my pocket.

I found Jacques working in a wheat field, his thin adolescent frame bent over the young stalks. He stood up and hugged me with tears glistening in his eyes. We had not seen each other in many months. He was eighteen but looked older, with dark shadows under his eyes and a serious gaze.

Jacques and I had a special sibling bond. We thought and felt alike and suffered from the same emotional and physical ailments. We both dreamed about studying music. Jacques loved the Russian mandolin while I preferred the violin. When we were growing up in Dereczyn, during the time when Papa was living in France, Mama often lacked nutritious food to give us and we frequently felt extreme weakness when we exerted ourselves too much. Whenever we were out walking in the hot sun, we would often feel pain and sudden fatigue that made it almost impossible to stand up. When we forced ourselves to reach our destination, we would collapse and cry hysterically. Then we needed a meal and complete rest to be revived.

I remembered a story Mama had told us about Jacques when he was a very young child. It was a very cold winter in Dereczyn and Jacques, who was no more than three or four years old, became seriously ill. Mama could not afford to take him to see a doctor. Jacques suddenly stopped breathing. A neighbor, hearing

Mama's scream, rushed inside our house and stared, horrified, at the lifeless child. She ordered Mama to carry Jacques outside. The cold air somehow had revived him and caused him to start crying. His life was saved.

Jacques was a city boy who had never seen a cow, horse or pig before in his life. I could not imagine how he was making the adjustment to farm life. He was thrown into farm work as if he had been put on another planet. I knew that manual labor in the fields under a hot sun would make him sick.

He showed me the barn where he slept each night—a dilapidated building. Pigs burrowed themselves beneath piles of hay near an old straw mattress where he slept. We walked in silence outside and he told me about his daily routine. He was up before dawn each day to feed the pigs and tend the crops. Under a fiery summer sun and in the chill of late autumn, he labored each day in the fields and in the barn.

For Jacques, as for me in Le Guédeniau, even worse than the exhausting physical labor was the isolation. The farmers expected him to work very hard, as they did, each day, and he felt no camaraderie with the other men who labored in the fields. The family had lived and toiled on this farmland for generations and had hired very little help. Jacques was an outsider. Pork was served almost daily. For a while Jacques tried to survive on just bread and vegetables, but he learned to adapt to his surroundings and soon began eating non-kosher dishes. At least food there was fairly plentiful.

Jacques, like myself, was living a life of subterfuge. Each day he had to lie about his family, childhood, and religion. Afraid that he might inadvertently say something that would reveal his identity, he preferred to remain silent at the dinner table. Living a lie day after day took a toll on his health and well-being. Jacques was constantly on his guard, always wearing a mask. He missed his family, friends, and the life he had known in Paris before the war.

"*Et toi, Sarah, tu n'as pas bonne mine. Comment vas-tu?*"(Sarah, you don't look too well. How are you?) I told Jacques about my miserable life in Le Guédeniau, but did not say anything about my health. He frowned and put his arm around my shoulder. Then we smiled at the similarity of our situations: both of us alone and unsuited for our jobs. We had grown into adults before passing through adolescence. Before we could continue our conversation, I heard a growling sound that made me jump. A huge dog came running toward us, barking, and Jacques grabbed my arm to pull me into the barn. "That beast snarls at me and constantly tries to attack me. He bit me the first night I arrived and my leg still has a scar." He showed me an angry red mark on the back of his right leg.

We had little time for goodbyes. Both of us needed to return to work. I wanted to visit Jacques again soon. I knew he was depressed. As for me, I wondered how I could continue living in Le Guédeniau. Where else could I go?

CHAPTER 16

TRAVELING BACK TO PARIS,
SUMMER 1943

A LETTER ARRIVED ONE DAY from my older sister Paulette. She
and Maurice had just gotten married! Paulette and Maurice had
met two years ago, when Paulette was nineteen years old. While
attending High Holy Days services at our synagogue, we had
stepped outside during a break for some fresh air. It was early
September and the summer heat had not yet abated. Women
dressed in their best outfits were fanning themselves. Children,
looking uncomfortable in their tight-fitting, dressy clothes, chatted among friends in the courtyard. A middle-aged woman had
approached Mama and introduced herself. "Good day, *Madame*.
My son was sitting on the other side of the synagogue and he
noticed your beautiful daughter. Would you permit him to meet
her?" That was how it all began. As Mama said, "A match was
made in heaven."

I opened Paulette's letter and began to read:

> *Here in Paris, everyone lives in fear. There are frequent police
> raids and Jews have gone into hiding. Since the Vel d'Hiv rafle no
> one feels safe from deportation. I didn't know how Maurice and
> I would be able to have a wedding ceremony at City Hall with-
> out attracting the attention of the police. We went there sepa-
> rately, each of us taking a different street. My heart was pounding
> as I walked. I expected the police to stop me at each intersection.
> Somehow we made it and we had a short ceremony at the Mairie*

(city hall), followed by a service at the synagogue, led by Papa. It was just Mama, Papa, Maurice, and I. Of course we could not invite guests. Since Maurice also has an Ausweis, we will continue to live in Paris.

I remember hearing from Mama how Paris had changed. I would hardly recognize it, she'd said. The city was just a shadow of itself. She said that noisy, brazen Germans were everywhere in cafés and restaurants and they provided the main business for café owners. Food shortages were apparently much worse in Paris than in the countryside. Adolescents and adults were allowed smaller rations than young children, so everyone was always hungry. Mama spent hours waiting in lines outside grocery stores only to find nothing left on the shelves but a few dry loaves of bread and some canned goods. She said that lines started to form early in the morning every day. Coffee, cheese, eggs, and meat were no longer available in grocery stores. Since so many farmers were in prisoner-of-war camps, there was very little fresh produce. Women had the burden of running farms and they were also managing shops everywhere. Mama said that long food lines were creating riots. Apparently a crowd of 150 Parisians attacked a shopkeeper on Rue Daguerre when they accused her of selling rotten peaches.

Nobody wanted to have to buy or sell on the *marché noir* (black market), but it was impossible to avoid it. Whenever Claire brought home some cheese, milk, and eggs for Mama and Papa, Mama sold some of it to her neighbors so that she and Papa would have some money to buy other goods. Buying and selling ration coupons became a big business. A few Parisians were making fortunes on the black market, while many French people were fighting to stay alive.

Living in Paris was a daily struggle to survive. We heard about petty crimes and about bribes paid to shopkeepers to obtain extra food. Prices of food rose so unpredictably that bartering goods had replaced money. Some traded butter for a typewriter or cigarettes for a bicycle. Some opportunists profited from the Occupation; café owners and shopkeepers with a large German clientele became wealthy almost overnight.

I learned that when Mama and Papa had moved into their secret apartment, they had to move so quickly that they left almost everything behind. Mama went back later to get some food and other items. To avoid being stopped by the German police, she did not take the Métro. Instead, she walked the four miles to their new apartment carrying her heavy bundles!

I thought of the risks Mama faced every day when she went outside. She had to stay away from public squares, the Métro, and buses, where police made frequent identification checks. During her long waits at grocery stores, she had to speak as little as possible, since neighbors might notice her foreign accent and report her to the police. Mama was an easy target for the *Milice*.

Mama and Papa constantly worried that their non-Jewish neighbors would become suspicious of them and report them to the police. We heard stories of neighbors who took furniture and goods from the apartments of deported Jews in order to improve their own lot. Times were hard and compassion was at its lowest level. Mama and Papa shared an apartment with a Jewish couple who had a teenage son, Guy. Guy stayed inside day after day, trying to occupy himself with books and cards. He was restless and miserable. One day he told his parents he needed a breath of fresh air. He stepped outside to take a short walk and never returned. The *Milice* arrested him.

Claire told me that when she had arrived at Mama and Papa's secret apartment, the *concierge* had rushed outside to warn her that our parents had to leave right away. She was in danger of being denounced by neighbors who knew she was renting an apartment to Jews. "Please, *Madame*. Would you allow them to stay here just a little longer?" Claire had begged her. "Please. Their lives depend on it." The *concierge* had generously relented and allowed them to stay.

Claire wrote to me about another harrowing experience she'd had the previous month in Paris. She traveled regularly by train from her hiding place in Burgundy to Mama and Papa's apartment to bring them dairy products. It was a two-and-a-half-hour train ride from Rogny-les-Sept-Écluses to Paris and she made this trip every few weeks. One day when she'd arrived at the Métro station Gare de l'Est, German and French police officers were waiting at the exit, checking identification cards. By luck, it was a French officer who stopped Claire and asked her for identification. "I don't have any, *Monsieur*," Claire admitted, looking very distressed. The officer stared at her for a while. Claire was trembling and kept her gaze fixed on the ground. She was just fourteen years old. He then decided to let her go. From that moment on, Claire never took the Métro in Paris. Instead, she walked the extra miles to their apartment from a train station at the outskirts of the city. Claire said that if the German officer had stopped her, she would have been arrested immediately.

I thought about Mama's and Claire's bravery as they faced the daily dangers of Paris streets. Each time they walked outside, a police officer could stop them and ask for identification. Who knew if the police would accept their forged identification cards? But even those who never went outside were in danger: they could die of hunger in their apartments. Learning to survive in occupied France meant learning to adapt to the ever-changing rules of a harsh, deadly environment, to always be one step ahead of the Nazis.

Something else was needed for survival in Paris, though. Mama spoke to neighbors who knew Yiddish and she was able to communicate in broken French when it was important to understand what was happening. In our different Paris neighborhoods she was not an outsider any longer. She had made contacts with others. The bond of trust between *concierge* and tenants, between neighbors in the same building or on the street often made the difference between life and death.

At the end of Paulette's letter, I read a cryptic sentence that made my heart beat faster. She and Mama had read between the lines of my last letter and figured out I was ill and depressed in Le Guédeniau. "You must come back to Paris immediately, Sarah. We have found someone who we think can help you."

CHAPTER 17

THE "SIXIÈME,"
SUMMER 1943

A TALL, LIGHT-HAIRED MAN of about nineteen was waiting for me in Mama and Papa's apartment. I had just walked in, still shaken from my long train ride. By some miracle, no police officer had stopped me en route to inspect my forged identification card. Still, I had been unable to breathe freely until I reached the apartment at Place de la République.

"Sarah?" The handsome man extended his hand to me. "I'm Claude, Claude Gutmann, from the *Sixième*" (Sixth). He told me briefly about the underground organization he belonged to. The *Sixième* was an offshoot of the French Jewish Scout movement. I remembered spending a carefree week just before the war camping in the woods with the Jewish scouts, the "*éclaireurs juifs*." Paulette had contacted Claude and asked if he could produce a new false identification card and find a new hiding place for me. He was from Alsace-Lorraine, from an observant family. His calm presence began to put me at ease. To the fear in my eyes, Claude responded with a gentle smile. To Mama and Papa's look of apprehension, he explained that they need not worry. He said he would accompany me personally on a train to a "safe house" in Clermont-Ferrand, in central France.

"You must memorize your new name and address, in case we are questioned by the Gestapo or the *Milice*," Claude said. "You are now Suzanne Leblanc. We are keeping your original initials

'S' and 'L' to make it easier for you to remember your new identity." He showed me my forged identification card, which had been washed in chemicals to appear slightly aged. Under "religion," I read "*catholique.*" "The train trip will take about three and a half hours," he continued. "If stopped by the police, we will say we are two friends on a vacation trip to the countryside."

There was hardly time to speak to Mama and Papa. We had been separated for almost a year and I had grown into a young woman now. I basked in happiness at seeing them again, even briefly. They both looked thinner. I saw tears well up in Mama's eyes. I soon learned that the *Sixième* was a well-organized Resistance group with branches all over France. They were able to operate even in Paris, right under the noses of Germans. But time was of the essence, and we had to leave before the Gestapo noticed suspicious activity in our apartment. Mama and Papa's lives could be endangered.

The long train trip went smoothly. I gazed through the window at farmland in the Loire valley. Wheat fields and fruit orchards soon gave way to mountainous terrain as we entered the *Massif Central* area. I trembled as the train made a stop at Vichy, the seat of Pétain's government. Several French police officers boarded the train. They sat down in nearby seats and immediately began to talk loudly to each other, not glancing in our direction. Claude stared calmly out the window as if he were a tourist. As I looked down, I noticed that he wore wooden-soled shoes. Leather had become exorbitantly expensive since most leather goods were being shipped to Germany.

As exhausted as I was when we finally arrived safely at Clermont-Ferrand, I had to stare at my new home with wonder. Majestic volcanic mountains encircled the city, which slumbered in a blue haze. We had to walk quite a distance up a hill to reach the "safe house." I began to feel faint, not having eaten anything since the morning. My whole body was aching. It was the same condition I had known since early childhood, a feeling of weakness whenever I exerted myself. I asked Claude to stop for a moment so that I could catch my breath. He waited patiently with me. We admired the dark gray Gothic cathedral with its soaring spires. Claude told me that it was constructed from hardened volcanic lava.

The "safe house," as Claude called it, was a busy apartment where other leaders of the *Sixième* met. Some were bringing children in transit, on their way to another safe house. Some, like Claude, were bringing children there to stay. Claude introduced me to a group of teenagers, girls and boys living together like a family. Claude, before leaving, said he would check on me regularly and would try to find a job for me in the city.

Dinner was served simply, family-style, at a large table. Since the *Sixième* had limited resources and since food was strictly rationed, we had to be content with a scant meal of bread and vegetables. In spite of this, I soon found myself smiling and joking at the table. I was among friends of my age for the first time in many years. After dinner, Clara, a seventeen-year-old girl who was orphaned at the beginning of the war, showed me her small record collection and played her favorite opera, Bizet's "Carmen." She sang along with Carmen's famous aria, "Habañera." I admired her beautiful, clear soprano voice. "You must be thinking about becoming a singer," I told her.

I learned more about the *Sixième* from Clara, and we became close friends. The brave leaders were Jewish *éclaireurs* (scouts), also known as E.I.F., who took their motto "Service" very seriously. Young adults of eighteen to twenty years old, girls and boys only slightly older than us, fought without any weapons and traveled the length and breadth of France in search of hiding places for Jewish adolescents. It was work that was anonymous and extremely dangerous.

The story of how this group of eighty-eight young adults became an underground organization was an amazing one. In November 1941 the Vichy government had created the organization U.G.I.F. (Union of French Jews) to coordinate all Jewish activities in France. The *Sixième* (Sixth) was part of this organization under official Vichy control. "Sixth" referred to the sixth department, reserved for youth. By funding Jewish social welfare projects at the beginning of the Occupation, the Nazis were forcing Jews into involuntary collaboration through their record-keeping. The Gestapo would later use the lists provided by U.G.I.F. to try to locate the children and deport them.

Clara said that the previous summer, some French police officials who were sympathetic to the Jewish scouts warned a group of boy scouts in southwestern France about impending roundups of young foreign Jews. The scouts in the small village of Moissac immediately dissolved the scout camps and focused all their efforts on rescuing Jewish adolescents. Then, they created laboratories for producing false identification cards. Moissac became the center for the underground movement known as the "*Sixième*" and the Gestapo were always trying to hunt them down. The organization quickly proceeded to branch out, dividing the unoccupied zone into seven different regions. Each region had its own director and assistants. The leaders of the *Sixième* were able to use records available in the Vichy-controlled agency to track down children and rescue them before the Gestapo could deport them. Sadly, the Gestapo reached some U.G.I.F. children before the *Sixième* could save them.

While other Resistance groups such as the O.S.E., a Jewish child welfare organization, worked to hide and care for young children, the *Sixième* devoted itself primarily to rescuing adolescents. This group had even organized escape routes for Jews to cross the borders into Switzerland and Spain! They also recruited volunteers to fight in the *maquis* (underground combatant army) and to rejoin the Allied armies.

Clara and I spent hours talking about our dreams for the future, when the war would finally be over. We spoke about boys, romance, school, and music. She told me about her parents, who had been killed in a bombing attack early in the war. She did not have any brothers or sisters, so she listened intently to tales about my large family.

We celebrated everyone's birthday at the safe house with special "gifts." When a boy named Matt turned sixteen, he received a large, colorfully wrapped box. He opened it very excitedly. He found a smaller box inside the large box, and then another smaller box inside this one. He kept opening one box after another, until he came to a very small package. In it were two pieces of hard sugar, a very rare item during the war. Then we all laughed and sang "Happy Birthday!"

Claude Gutmann came by our apartment regularly to see how all of us were doing. He would tell us about the daring actions undertaken by members of the *Sixième* to save Jews from the Gestapo. I realized how lucky I was to be there.

Thanks to my new forged identification card, Claude was able to find a job for me in a large store in the center of town. I would be working at a hardware store selling seeds, farming tools, and other basic goods. The owner of the store had no idea that I was Jewish. Had he known this, he certainly would not have hired me. Claude also warned me about a potential problem: German soldiers came frequently to this store.

CHAPTER 18

HIDING IN CLERMONT-FERRAND, 1943–1944

I LEARNED, WITH CLAUDE'S HELP, to serve French and German clientele. The owner of the hardware store, Monsieur Olivier, instructed me well and kept a close eye on me. I, who had been unable to lie when I had first arrived in Le Guédeniau the previous year, was finally mastering my role. During the day I was Suzanne Leblanc, a polite, efficient French salesclerk. My French was fluent and I blended in well with other store help. I assisted French farmers and German soldiers who were purchasing gardening supplies to send home to their families. The Germans asked questions about the differences between different tools and seeds, speaking obsequiously in broken French. I answered them all calmly, hiding my fears.

In the evenings, back in my apartment, I became Sarah Lew again. I thrived in the warm, congenial atmosphere of our safe house. When I flirted with teenage boys like Matt and Jérome or confided secrets to Clara, the war receded from my thoughts. I became a teenager again and my health soon improved. We shared kitchen chores and swept our rooms each evening. Clara and I sometimes sang together and listened to operas. We dreamed about our future in a free country and talked about going back to school. I thought about saving up for a violin of my own. I read novels that were in our common room. Russian novels with romantic plots were my favorites. Claude stopped by regularly to inquire about our jobs and our well-being.

The BBC radio broadcasts from London brought some good news about the war. The Russian army was advancing in Europe and had already liberated Kiev. Italy had surrendered to the Allies. The area in southeastern France occupied by Italy became an island of security for Jews in Vichy France, since the Italians refused to deport Jews who took refuge there. When news reached Paris of this haven, thousands of Jews fled there from the capital and all parts of France.

Claude kept us informed of rescue work undertaken by the *Sixième*. The group had just created an adult division to help older Jews cross the borders into Switzerland and Spain. "Adults are much more difficult to hide," Claude said. "The foreigners, especially recent refugees to France, are not able to speak French. How are they to be camouflaged? That is why we need to find escape routes out of France for them immediately. Recently, we escorted a Polish rabbi, his wife, and seven children to the Spanish border. We had to cut off the rabbi's beard, give him a Basque beret, and, to complete the deception, make him a deaf-mute. He played his role well and they all made it safely across!"

We learned how the *Sixième* and other activist groups had found hiding places for Jews in the most unexpected places. The nuns of Our Lady of Sion hid them in convents in Paris, Grenoble, and Marseille. The head nurse at a Toulouse hospital accepted them as patients until they could find a permanent refuge. The most bizarre hiding place of all was a leper clinic, where the Protestant director assisted Jews in their escape.

Claude said that the *Sixième* was indebted to Protestant and Catholic clergy for their aid. The Bishop of Nice, Monsignor Rémond, had established a Resistance network which hid more than five hundred Jewish children in Catholic schools. The Jesuit priest Pierre Chaillet was also at the forefront of rescue efforts for Jews. He helped to establish *L'Amitié Chrétienne* (Christian Friendship) to save victims of the Vichy regime, especially Jews.

According to Claude, when the Vichy Commissioner for Jewish Affairs dissolved the Jewish Scout movement the previous year, the *Sixième* intensified its underground work. The leader of the Jewish Scouts, Robert Gamzon, started a band of Resistance fighters in southeastern France that called themselves *Maquisards*, named for the *maquis* (bushes) where they hid in mountainous regions. Leaders of the *Sixième* took great risks to save Jewish children and adults. They could be arrested at any time. Claude did not want to speak about those who had been arrested and we did not dare ask.

My thoughts often returned to Paris, to Mama and Papa. How were they managing to survive in that city, where the Gestapo were arresting Jews at such an alarming rate? Claire told me that whenever she traveled to Paris to bring our parents dairy products, she saw people on bicycles scouring the countryside for food and bartering whatever they could. Everyone had to use the *Système D* (resourcefulness), as they called it, to get by when life in Vichy France became unbearable.

Each evening, our group of teenagers gathered around a small radio to hear the latest war news. By spring 1944, the Allies were bombing German targets heavily across Europe and the tide of the war was turning in their favor. There were rumors that there would soon be an Allied land invasion of France. We were getting excited and hopeful. Perhaps I would be able to return to Paris before long. As the German army was suffering more losses, Resistance groups in France were growing bolder. We read in a clandestine newspaper that a communist group was sabotaging German factories in Paris and attacking German targets everywhere across France.

Resistance fighters were successful in assassinating several Nazi leaders, attacks to which Germany disproportionately responded.

For each German killed, the Gestapo captured and killed a hundred hostages. They seized people in street raids and in hotels and restaurants. It was a deadly cycle of violence that was becoming more terrifying each day. Since some Vichy officials were beginning to side with Resistance leaders and could no longer be trusted by Germany, the Nazis were quick to crush any inkling of a rebellion with an iron fist. We did not dare spend much time outdoors. Each of us walked quickly from the stores where we worked to the apartment.

My boss at the hardware store, Monsieur Olivier, had a young teenage son, Paul. One day, Paul went out and was unexpectedly arrested by the Gestapo. Monsieur Olivier ran to the German authorities, begging them to release him. He spoke to every German officer he could find, pleading and offering bribes. I saw him weeping inconsolably in the store. All that the German officers would tell him was that his son had already been deported to Germany.

In April, Claude came to warn us that our "safe house" was no longer safe. Some neighbors were becoming suspicious of movements in our apartment and he said they might betray us to the police. The Gestapo was becoming more ruthless every day and needed to fill their convoys to camps in Eastern Europe. I thought of Hélène's husband Jack, who had been deported by the Gestapo the previous year. I wondered if I would ever see him again.

The *Sixième* had plans for our escape, but we had to make a difficult choice. Claude would find a leader to take our group by train to the Swiss border, where another guide would help us cross into Switzerland. However, this was a risky plan since the Germans carefully patrolled the border with dogs. We would have to climb a barbed wire fence to escape into Switzerland. Recently, a group had tried to cross the Swiss border and had been arrested by the German police. The other choice would be to hide in a convent nearby. Several nuns had agreed to accept children from our safe house and protect them from the police.

Clara and I stared at each other without speaking. Which escape plan would we choose?

CHAPTER 19

SWITZERLAND, 1944

I DECIDED TO JOIN the group of teenagers escaping into Switzerland. Clara chose to hide in a convent. The risks of the border crossing and of the barbed wire fence were frightening to her. Our departure was planned for very early the next morning. Clara and I embraced. We hoped to see each other again in Paris when the war was over, but so many uncertainties hung over us. Claude would help us to stay in touch with one another, we were sure, but he had many dangerous rescue missions ahead of him.

A leader from the *Sixième* reviewed instructions with us carefully. We were pretending to be a group of students on a vacation trip with their teacher. We would carry no luggage, only what we could wear. I put on two dresses and an extra set of underwear and socks. My layers of clothing felt warm and tight, but fortunately the temperature was mild on this day in early May. We would ride a train together to a town next to the Swiss border, Annemasse. If stopped by police along the way, we would show our forged identification cards and let our leader do the talking for us. In Annemasse, we would meet another guide who would lead us to the border.

As we rode in silence on the train, I gazed at Clermont-Ferrand one last time to etch it in my memory. The city slept in a morning haze, encircled by bluish volcanic mountains. Just beyond the buildings with their orange-tiled roofs was the soaring

Gothic cathedral. Clara was on her way now to her new hiding place. I had barely been able to swallow a few morsels of dry bread for breakfast and to gulp down hot milk. I had no time to say goodbye to Claude or thank him. With our brave guide's presence on the train, though, I felt more excited than anxious. I thought again about Claude, who had made it possible for me to start a new life.

We reached the border town without incident. The sun had barely risen, so the light was dim and the air was hazy. Everything seemed enveloped in an opaque cloud. Our new guide met us and silently and hurriedly escorted us to a house close to the Swiss border. We could see across a field that there was a high fence straight ahead of us. Our guide explained rapidly that German soldiers were patrolling the border with dogs, and that there were intervals of a few minutes between their rounds at this border spot. He told us to be very quiet and to try to ignore the barking of dogs, since there was nothing we could do about this. He looked at our group of twelve children. Two of them were younger and smaller and would need help getting across.. "You must climb over the barbed wire fence as quickly as possible, helping the two small children. You must not stop at any moment, even if you are cut by wire. Just jump over and run as fast as you can. You will be safe on the other side." I looked around a moment later and saw that our leader had disappeared.

The next few instants passed in a fog. I don't remember thinking or feeling. Call it survival instinct—some special strength stored away for a moment when your life is at risk. We were alone, facing the barbed wire fence. I saw the fearful eyes of a small girl next to me, standing motionless as if transfixed. I could hear dogs barking, their sounds getting closer. I lifted the little girl and helped her onto the fence. Then I began climbing behind her and helped her to the top, pushing her over the fence just before

I jumped to the ground. Suddenly we were all on the other side, lying dazed and speechless in the grass.

I looked at my hands and legs, bloody from the barbs on the fence, but did not notice the pain. My clothes were torn and also bloodied. The little girl moved closer to me. We were safe at last. It was a different world, a meadow with flowers and tall grass. We must have been in shock, because none of us could move for a few moments. As our eyes began to focus on the surroundings, we saw a farm nearby. The morning light was getting brighter. All at once, out of nowhere came two well-fed blond children with long braids who came up and observed us. They did not say a word but I felt from their look that they saw us as weird animals. . . not to touch. Within minutes, they turned around and ran toward their house, out of sight.

Soon after that, two Swiss police officers were in front of us with orders to stand up and follow them. We rode a bus through little villages and towns; our eyes wide open, not feeling hunger or pain. The ride must have been quite long, but I was not aware of time passing. Cows were leisurely grazing in valleys, near farm-houses and neat, clean villages. Snow-covered mountains formed a backdrop to lush meadows. Everywhere I stared at picture-post-card views. When the bus stopped in a small town, we saw choco-late bars and imported sardines on display in a store. It all seemed like a fairy tale in a beautifully illustrated book.

The large refugee camp was in Soral, not far from Geneva. It was surrounded by a high fence. The only entryway was a tall wrought-iron gate guarded by Swiss police. We were met by authorities who told us that we were being quarantined for two months as a preventive measure against infectious diseases. Each of us was then interrogated by an administrator who prepared a file on us. What was my name? "Sarah Lew." Age? "Seventeen." Where was I from? "Dereczyn, Poland." Religion? "Jewish."

Observant or secular Jew? It took me a few moments to respond to this question. I thought of my strict religious upbringing and my years at the Hirsch School. I thought of Papa, who prayed to God all day. I had strayed from my religious upbringing while coping with daily survival and I didn't know how I felt about religion anymore. That was the first moment I had given it a thought. Mama had sent us kids to buy non-kosher cold cuts when the war began, knowing that children needed protein and that kosher food was not available. We had eaten it with our fingers outside our apartment. It had been a struggle to remain observant in occupied France. The administrator's question startled me and I needed to think more. Seeing the insistent look in his eyes, I answered, "Yes, I am an observant Jew." He wrote it down.

I followed kosher food laws strictly at first and avoided eating most of the food served at the camp. I found myself very often hungry. Then I slowly began to adapt to my new surroundings and tried some foods I had never been allowed to taste during my childhood.

We were each given a straw mattress to sleep on. Very soon after the first night, many of us noticed a skin infection on our arms and legs. We were itching all over. They took us in a van to a nearby hospital where we were told to enter by the back door, to the area reserved for non-Swiss residents. In a basement room, we were told to undress. Then some attendants sprayed a disinfectant all over our bodies as we stood naked. I trembled as men and women in white coats glared at us.

The refugee camp was teeming with adults and children from every country, both Jews and non-Jews fleeing the Nazis. Imagine my astonishment when I discovered my old friend Rosa in the crowd. I had not seen her in more than two years, almost an eternity ago. We embraced and stared at each other, wide-eyed. She told me that the O.S.E. had rescued her and had led her to the Swiss border. I had some difficulty recognizing her. Her face had lost its adolescent innocence. She had become an adult too quickly, like a flower forced to grow under harsh light. We chatted but left unsaid what was most on our minds: whether our families were out of danger.

Never before had I encountered so many people from different ways of life. It became an exhilarating experience: meeting others, learning to communicate, discovering. I felt that I was awakening after a slumber of five years, after thinking only about daily survival. When I turned eighteen years old in November, I believed that adult life was at last beginning for me.

As all of us stood in line in the large dining hall, carrying food trays and waiting to select our dinner dishes, I caught admiring glances of young men, refugees like myself. I basked in their long stares and returned their smiles. I had a glimpse of my reflection in the dining hall mirror and saw a graceful young woman staring back at me.

One Saturday morning I observed a young Jewish couple talking animatedly to each other while the woman washed her lingerie in a small basin. When she had finished, she hung her underwear on a line to dry. I looked at the two of them in total disbelief. Never before had I seen such intimacy between married people, certainly not in my parents' household. I looked up at the sky and told myself, "Now God will strike them dead as a punishment for working on the Sabbath." I was relieved to see that this did not happen. I had never thought until now that someone could be Jewish but not observant.

I discovered then that Jewish people could be completely different from each other and yet still consider themselves Jews. Some kept strictly kosher and were very observant. Others smoked on the Sabbath and happily ate whatever they were served, without worrying about whether or not it was kosher.

I began to question for the first time what it meant to be Jewish, something that Papa had never discussed.

CHAPTER 20

NEW PATHS,
SUMMER 1944–SPRING 1945

OUTSIDE OUR HAVEN in Switzerland, the war raged on. We caught news of battles from time to time in radio broadcasts and from leaders in our camp. The director of the refugee camp announced that the Allies had landed in Normandy on June 6. We all cheered and clapped at the news. Later that summer there was more good news about the war: the Allied army had arrived in southern France and they were sweeping through the country. By late August, Paris was liberated. We missed much of the news, however, since we did not have newspapers. We did not hear that the Gestapo had raided some U.G.I.F. children's homes and had deported hundreds of Jewish children, even as the German armies were in full retreat. Even the *Sixième* had been unable to save them. In the last few months of the war, the Nazi war machine knew no limits of the evil it could perpetrate: churches, synagogues, and houses were set on fire in France and entire populations of villages were massacred. Even just one week before the liberation of Paris, the Nazis continued to send packed cattle cars from Drancy to Auschwitz. I did not know then that Claude had perished on one of his daring rescue missions—he had been shot by German police during a raid.

We also later learned that a Jewish Resistance army had marched into Drancy on August 17, 1944, to free 1,523 remaining survivors threatened with deportation. Members of the French

Partisans and Jewish Resistance groups joined the Allies and the Free French Forces led by General de Gaulle to finally liberate France in January 1945. The war still continued to rage far beyond France's borders even after this nation had been freed. There were fierce battles against the Japanese in the Pacific. The longest battle of the war, the *Bataille des Ardennes,* (Battle of the Bulge) would occur in the winter of 1944–1945. It took the lives of about 19,000 Americans and 1,400 British soldiers. We refugees at Soral knew little, if anything, of the terrible battles being fought, or of the number of human lives this unspeakable tragedy was claiming.

Our camp director announced in the fall that they were looking for young women as volunteers to go to a nursing school in Vevey, near Montreux, Switzerland. We would get training in pediatric nursing to help refugee women and their newborns at a clinic recently created there. The building, a former resort near Lake Léman, would have good accommodations for those who volunteered. I agreed to join the group of volunteers, mainly because of the chance to leave my overcrowded quarters at Soral and to gain new work experience. I knew nothing at all about nursing. Getting an education had a strong appeal to me, though. School meant exploring new fields, working with others, escaping from my own narrow world.

A French psychiatrist, Dr. Pugatz, who was a refugee like us, visited our camp to talk about the struggle in Palestine to create a Jewish nation. He taught us about our Jewish heritage and told us that in Palestine they would need many young Jews like ourselves to help build Israel. We learned some Hebrew songs and he showed us how to dance the *hora.* Rosa and I listened with great interest and joined other refugees in a large circle. We began to sway and leap to the dance's joyful rhythm and found ourselves captivated by the dance's pulsing beat.

Soon after volunteering to go to nursing school, I was taken by bus with other young women to a large converted resort called *Home les Terrasses* on the shores of Lake Léman. My room had a quilt-covered bed, a large window with lace curtains, a chest of drawers and a private shower, something I had always dreamed of having in Paris. We soon settled into our routine: four hours each morning of nursing instruction (taught in French by Swiss doctors and nurses), followed by lunch. In the afternoon, we had cleaning duty in the clinic and then a nursing internship: we were each assigned to a mother and her newborn baby. We worked in shifts; sometimes I worked through the night, and then found myself struggling to get through the next day—groggy, red-eyed, unable to sleep because of bright sunlight and continual noise.

I fell in love with the twin babies born to a Hungarian Jewish woman. I showed her how to care for her baby boys and I checked their body weight and vital signs each afternoon. When the new mother was about to leave our clinic, she came over to say good-bye to me and I found myself choking up with tears.

My first exposure to sickness and death in a setting removed from war was at *Home les Terrasses*. I already knew about cruelty and violence, but I knew nothing before now about young babies and children who often died from natural causes, even after doctors and nurses had fought hard to save them. During one of my night shifts, I saw a young Italian mother who had just lost her baby to illness. She was hysterical. She shrieked and held her baby tightly in her arms, crying uncontrollably and refusing to let go of her dead child. An Italian friend of mine translated her hysterical words. She was blaming her Jewish mother-in-law for casting an evil spell on her baby.

Our cleaning duty at the hospital was very laborious. We scrubbed each hospital room thoroughly. We had to mop floors with a strong detergent and then we had to apply wax to the wooden floors with our bare hands. Before long my hands developed blisters and an allergic reaction to the floor polish. A doctor gave me a cream that soon healed my skin condition.

One Sunday after dinner, the camp administrator asked if a volunteer would please read aloud a letter from the French Embassy. The letter announced that France had been liberated by the Allies and Free French Forces. I remained silent. The girl next to me yelled out to the administrator, pointing to me, that I knew French very well and would be able to read it. I responded shyly, "No, thank you," but wanted to say, "Yes, I will read it." I could feel my heart pounding and my face turning red. For just once, I could be the center of attention, but I continued to remain quiet while seething inside for not having the courage to speak out in public.

On evenings after dinner when I did not have a night shift, there was plenty of time for socializing with my new international friends. A group of Italian girls became friendly with me. We joked and chatted using sign language and words taken from several languages, since none of us could speak each other's languages. I joined them in singing sessions. As Christmas was approaching, a group of women came up to me and one asked if I would like to join a small chorus singing Christmas carols, accompanied by a pianist. It would be very festive and enjoyable. I hesitated for a moment. "You know, I am Jewish and I don't know any of these songs," I said. "Don't worry," she replied. "We can certainly teach you the words." Since I loved singing and realized that I liked the idea of being a star, I told her I would join the group. A day later, word had gotten out that I would be singing Christmas carols. A group of Jewish women came up to speak to me, and one of them was furious. "What is wrong with you, Sarah? You have agreed to sing Christmas carols? Have you forgotten what Christians have been doing to Jews?" I decided reluctantly not to sing.

A tall, dashing older man seemed to take a particular interest in me. He introduced himself as Boris. He was Russian, but he had lived in France until the war broke out. He was working at the clinic doing odd jobs: repairing broken plumbing and installing equipment. He told me that I would enjoy seeing his magic show, which he would someday perform for us. I did not know whether to believe him or not, but found him fascinating anyway.

Boris talked about his daughter who was my age. I enjoyed his charming manners and his sophistication. He said that I was the first Jew he had ever met. He had grown up with anti-Semitic ideas, but since meeting me he had changed his attitude.

After our classes had ended, we organized a "graduation" party. I decided to write to Boris, who was by then working in a Geneva nightclub. I invited him to our party. To our astonishment, Boris put on an amazing magic show. Standing on an improvised stage, he wore an elegant black tuxedo with a long cape. With great dexterity, he waved his cape and made objects disappear and reappear in the wink of the eye. Out of a cloud of gray smoke flew two white doves that flapped their wings and went soaring over the stage into the audience.

On another weekend, two young Italian boys invited me to go for a canoe ride with them. I accepted, although after some hesitation, since I had never been in a canoe before. They began immediately to sing very loudly in Italian, all the while joking with me, as we canoed in Lake Léman. I just kept praying that I would get my feet back on solid ground again, since I was terrified of deep water. We all made it back somehow.

One day as I sat on a bench facing Lake Léman, an Englishman struck up a conversation with me. George, as he called himself, was the Consul of Crete and a war refugee like myself. Like Boris, he was an older man, very gallant and charming. When we got to know each other better, he brought me pastries, and once he took me out to an elegant restaurant where everyone but me wore very stylish, expensive clothes. I could feel the cold glances of chic, worldly clients as they stared at my plain drab dress and worn shoes.

After our evening out, I returned to find the front door of *Home les Terrasses* locked. I rang the doorbell twice and no one responded. I had missed the strict ten p.m. curfew! What was I going to do? I had to find shelter until the morning. I didn't see any other building nearby on the hilltop. Then I noticed the clinic's garage, where baby carriages were stored. I walked inside and climbed into a baby carriage with great difficulty. I somehow managed to fall sleep, curled up tightly inside. But not for long! I fell out of it and the carriage landed on top of me. It was very cold and I spent the rest of the night shivering. When the side door finally opened at six a.m., to let in maintenance staff, I crept inside like a thief.

As soon as George learned that the Allies had liberated Crete, he stopped by to say goodbye to me. The camp director refused to allow him to visit me, but he left me a sweet note with some delicious pastries.

One evening, our camp director announced that the war had finally ended. Europe was free at last. The directors would assist each of us in getting repatriated. Everyone in the room began clapping, screaming, and shrieking. We stood up and spontaneously started to dance, then hugged one another. Many people were weeping. I would be going home to Paris at last! I wrote to my parents at their old address, at 80 Rue Doudeauville. Were they still alive and well? What had become of my family and of all my old friends? I did not know what to expect.

CHAPTER 21

LIBERATION, PARIS, 1945

ON MAY 15, 1945, I stepped off the train at Gare du Nord in Paris and found my family standing on the station platform, waiting for me. We stared at each other in disbelief for a few seconds before falling into one another's arms in tears. Everyone had changed so dramatically that we were at a loss for words. It was a miracle that we were still alive after four years of Nazi Occupation. Claire had become a woman and Madeleine, a tall, graceful adolescent. Max had grown from a toddler into a handsome boy. Bernard and Jacques had both become grown men. Jacques wore a military uniform and looked rugged and manly. He told me that he had joined the *maquis* and had run away from the farm to fight in the Resistance. Mama looked older with her gray hair, but her smile was as warm as I had remembered it. Papa, serious, quiet and reserved as always, had a more somber expression than before. Hélène and Paulette, who lived further away, could not be there at the station, but they joined us later. From everyone's surprised gaze, I felt that they were trying to adjust to me as well.

Mama and Papa had moved back to their old apartment at 80 Rue Doudeauville. The intense joy of our reunion gave way to shock when I stepped into our apartment. Everything had been ransacked and looted. The rooms had been gutted: furniture, light fixtures, built-ins, and all. Mama and Papa had quickly bought a few second-hand pieces of furniture, but the place had a barren, desolate air. When our building superintendent, Monsieur Auber, saw us enter the apartment, he frowned and looked surprised, as if he were expecting us to not come back. To him, we were intruders whom he would be forced to tolerate. After so many years of being away, it disturbed me that there was still no running water or heat in the apartment. My stay in Switzerland had completely changed my perspective on what constituted an acceptable apartment. 80 Rue Doudeauville truly belonged to an earlier century. My family deserved better than that, I thought.

Without even hesitating, I knocked on Monsieur Auber's door the next day. He partially opened the door and recoiled as if I carried a contagious disease, clearly taken aback by my sudden appearance. "Monsieur Auber," I began. "We have been good tenants here for many years. We would like to see some improvements in the apartment. Since there is already running water in the hallway, why can't we have a faucet with running water in our own apartment? Why can't we have heat in our apartment? These are not adjustments that would be very difficult to accomplish."

"Mademoiselle Lew," he said, choosing his words with a forced politeness that did not conceal his disdain. "There is simply nothing that can be done, I assure you." He glared at me and quickly closed his door before I could reply.

Paris looked ravaged after four years of Nazi pillaging. It was astonishing to see that the city was still intact, though. Paris, at long last liberated. With torn banners and posters lying on the streets, after recent parades welcoming the victorious Allied troops, the city was awakening with a post-war hangover. Stores were depleted of goods and the economy was in shambles. Charles de Gaulle had become President of the Provisional French Government. Without delaying, he had abolished all the anti-Jewish Vichy laws and had granted French Jews full citizenship once again. The new government promised to reinstate Jews in their former jobs, and to restore property to them that had been

"Aryanized" during the Occupation. For the present moment, though, everything was still in flux. Some neighbors were dismayed to see Jews returning to reclaim their old apartments and their former employment positions.

The French Jewish community was in complete disarray, having lost a third of its rabbis and closed all Jewish schools during the Occupation. Mama and Papa wanted Max to receive a Jewish education, but there were no classes available anywhere. They realized then that there was only one possible option: to have Max stay at a Jewish orphanage for a while, where he would have religious instruction. Poor Max was in tears but went along anyway with their plan.

The orphanage, quite far from Paris, was in a drab, ancient building. Mama noticed that the children there seldom laughed or played happily in groups; they were quiet and withdrawn. Having lost their parents in the war, they felt threatened by unseen dangers. I went with Mama once to visit Max. He said that he hated the food and missed home. Every Sunday, Mama would take a train to visit him, bringing him a package of his favorite home cooked foods. She tried to explain to him that the separation was necessary and would not last long.

Hélène, Paulette, and Maurice came to visit us shortly after my arrival home. Hélène was holding the hand of her little girl, Simone. Her forlorn expression told me what I had feared: Jack had not returned home from deportation. Hélène later shared some details with me. A friend who was a survivor of a death camp had seen Jack in a very weakened condition, shortly before his death. He died in Auschwitz.

Paulette and Maurice were holding a baby I had not met before, a boy named Michel. I learned about Paulette's difficult childbirth and their narrow escape to Clermont-Ferrand in late 1944:

"With the war raging and all the risks of getting deported, I was frightened when I discovered that I was pregnant," she told me. "I went to a pharmacy and got some pills to abort the baby. There were no doctors I could see and I was in hiding. I didn't know what else to do. I was afraid of being deported immediately, along with my baby, if I gave birth at a hospital. The pills gave me a terrible stomachache. Maurice's father saw the state I was in and immediately threw away the bottle of pills. After that, I managed to complete the pregnancy without having any doctor's examinations. A midwife came to my secret apartment at Place de la République when I went into labor. It was too dangerous to make noise so I bit my arm until it bled and lost a lot of blood during the delivery. When Michel was born, the midwife held him up by his feet to shake him and to untangle the cord that was strangling him. Thank God he is a fine, healthy baby."

Paulette told me that she and Maurice were not able to feed Michel properly, since they had no milk or food ration coupons. While she was nursing him she developed an infection and the baby came down with a fever. By late 1944 they were also in grave danger of being arrested because their *Ausweis* was no longer valid. She had sold a pair of sheets and Papa's leather boots on the black market and then they contacted the *Sixième*. With help from this Resistance organization, they were able to take a train to a village near Clermont-Ferrand. Maurice worked on a farm as a laborer and they stayed there safely until the end of the war. He secretly milked a cow so that he would be able to bring Paulette fresh milk each day to feed their baby. I did not realize until then that they had been living so close while I was in my safe house in Clermont-Ferrand.

It was some months later that we finally learned the fate of our old friends and neighbors from Paris and from Dereczyn, Poland. Surviving deportees, skeletal and hollow-eyed, were returning home from the war, haunted by what they had witnessed and experienced. What shocked us the most was how few people returned alive from the camps. Orphaned children, so many of them, were being housed in newly created orphanages all around France. The Lutétia Hotel was converted into a residence in Paris for surviving deportees without families or homes.

Although France had been liberated, the Vichy years had not yet been exorcised from the memory of all who had lived through them. A consensus settled in the nation as a whole to not speak of the Occupation or of deportations. If words such as "Auschwitz," "death camps," "gas chambers" sometimes crept into newspaper accounts, French people could not yet speak openly of these horrors. Many surviving Jews simply wished to become invisible, to blend in. Some Jews were changing their last names to sound more French, to make it harder for others to differentiate them from the rest of the population.

From an old friend of Hélène's, we learned that the entire population of Dereczyn had been marched into the woods by the Nazis. The men were made to dig large graves and everyone had to undress. Then they were all shot standing in front of these graves. Hélène's friend had somehow survived the shooting. He heard moaning all around him in the pit and realized that he was bleeding and wounded but still alive. The sky was becoming somber and the killers with their local helpers hurried to finish their job and leave. In the dark of night, he managed to crawl out of the pit. He survived in the woods by stealing food from nearby farms at night. One other couple had also hidden in the woods and had survived the war. They had a baby who died of malnutrition just before the Liberation. Dereczyn was nothing but a memory now.

Rosa learned that both her parents and her brother had died in Polish death camps. Only she and her older sister had survived. She told me in a broken voice that when she had returned to Paris, she had found her apartment looted. There was not even a trace left behind of her beloved family. Everything had been stolen or destroyed, including her younger brother's cherished violin.

A former roommate from our safe house in Clermont-Ferrand had learned of Claude's death, and also of the fate of Clara, my friend with the beautiful soprano voice who had hidden in a convent. The nuns had persuaded her to convert to Catholicism and then to become a nun, in order to save the souls of her dead parents. If she became a good Catholic, they told her, her parents' souls would go up to heaven, instead of burning in hell.

Mama learned that our elderly neighbor, whose granddaughter had given me piano lessons before the war, had died in Auschwitz along with her only granddaughter. Their apartment too had been pillaged and their beautiful piano stolen.

"Why, Papa?" I asked my father, who was back in his chair in the dining room, reading his prayer books. Papa looked up at me, startled by my question. "Why did so many Jews die?" I asked. "How did God let this happen?"

"Sarah, we do not question the Almighty's will. Only God knows why evil exists. We must obey the commandments God has given us and be good Jews."

"Millions of Jews, innocent people, so many children—died. I can't understand why God allowed it to happen."

"Sarah," Papa said, looking at me sadly. "I see that Switzerland has changed you." He turned back to his prayer book and became silent again. We did not discuss it any further.

Each Saturday morning, Papa went to synagogue and often stayed there afterward to chat with surviving members of his *shul*. I often saw him walking into our apartment later, looking serious and subdued, sitting down quietly in his armchair.

CHAPTER 22

PARIS, 1945–1948 AND MARSEILLE, 1948

I SHOWED MAMA AND PAPA the nursing certificate I had received in Switzerland. The certificate meant that I was qualified for a pediatric nursing position in a hospital. Papa said nothing, while Mama smiled and shook her head slightly. "Sarah, being a nurse is like being a maid in a hospital. Soon you will meet a young man, get married and have children of your own. That will be better than being a maid to someone else's child."

Strangely, I did not feel hurt by Mama's advice because I secretly agreed with her. Nursing had not been my own choice of a profession. The truth was that I had struggled through night shifts at the hospital and had felt very distressed by the sickness and death of babies.

I needed to think more about my future. I was eighteen years old, living at last in a free nation. I could settle down right away and get married like Mama had done when she was my age. Both Mama and Hélène had arranged marriages, but times were slowly changing for women. I could have a say in the choice of the man I would marry. I even read that women now had the right to vote in France.

Mama and my older sisters began to play matchmaker for me. But where were the handsome, educated young men of my dreams? So many had been murdered. Most survivors had no formal education and they had little ambition. The young men

Hélène and Paulette arranged for me to meet were in the clothing business, like themselves. We did not have much in common to talk about. Mama and Papa did not push me to meet a strictly observant Jew. Both of them knew that since I had returned from Switzerland I had my own ideas about life and religion.

I understood then that dreams and reality were two different worlds that could never meet. In my dreams I was an accomplished violinist, performing at recitals, playing music that stirred the soul. I could still hear those melodies in my head from early childhood, from gypsy violinists who played on the town square in Dereczyn, near my open window. In my dreams I was educated and accomplished, with a college diploma, like the men I admired. In reality, though, I was a woman, and I knew that women could choose to be teachers, nurses, secretaries, or housewives. In reality, I just had a primary school certificate and my parents were poor. Continuing higher education for a professional outcome in years to come? A dream world. Just as it was a dream to imagine a woman as doctor, prime minister, or virtuoso violinist. I knew better than to live in a dream world, although I would always be a dreamer at heart. My childhood had ended years ago.

Papa soon found a job for me through one of his friends. I worked as a clerk in a lawyer's office. My job consisted of entering accounting figures into a ledger and doing other clerical duties. With my parents' blessing I opened a savings account in my own name, and began depositing my paychecks in it. They wanted me to save for my future.

I shared an office with two women who joked constantly about married life. Once a month, I took the Métro to the accountant's office, to hand-deliver his cash payment. That was the best part of my job. I could read for forty-five minutes, uninterrupted, as I traveled. I had plenty of time for reading and daydreaming. I knew, however, that I wanted more than that for my career.

One day I saw a hand-written advertisement pasted on an office window: "Learn typing and stenography." I decided to follow through. I took the Métro to Place Pigalle, to the address listed in the advertisement. The neighborhood was a scene of strange contrasts. Famous nightclubs with their alluring lights and garish posters announcing upcoming shows stood near shabby, dilapidated buildings inhabited by the poor. Further down the street were hideaways where shady dealings of the underworld took place. I arrived at the home of Mademoiselle Thérelles, a middle-aged retired teacher who lived alone in a dark, cramped apartment filled with clutter. On one side table, however, sat a shiny new typewriter that caught my eye. I decided then to take lessons from her at night.

Mademoiselle Thérelles was a strict but good teacher and I learned quickly. Several months later, as I skimmed the daily newspaper, I saw a "Help Wanted" ad that read, "Secretary needed for clothing manufacturer in Paris." I gathered my courage, applied, and was hired on the spot. My boss was short and thick-set, with a temper. He yelled and terrified his staff, but treated me with respect as his private secretary.

My family soon settled into its old routine, but found the economic recovery in post-war France to be maddeningly slow. Papa resumed his functions at the synagogue as rabbi, teacher, and *shamas*. At home I sometimes saw him looking pensive and dejected. He did not speak to me about thoughts that must have troubled him.

Mama went back to being her spirited, hardworking old self, as before the war, devoting herself to our family of eight children minus the two who were now married. She took the Métro regularly to Les Halles market, where she could buy a sack of potatoes for a few pennies less than anywhere else. We often walked together to neighborhood open-air markets for fresh produce. She went to bargain stores to find dishes and cutlery for our apartment, and came home one day with two mismatched candle-sticks, one taller than the other. I overheard her singing to herself again. She resumed reading Jewish newspapers, especially enjoying romantic serial novels. She still loved going to the Yiddish theater whenever she had the chance. Claire, Mama, and I went once to Place de la République to see Molly Picon, the famous American actress and great star of the Yiddish theater. The audience applauded wildly and enthusiastically, but no one applauded as much as Mama did.

Our apartment still had no heat or hot water and the bathroom was in the hallway. It was difficult to do without running water in the kitchen. Monsieur Auber was indifferent to tenants' needs and kept his distance from us. We still had ugly, second-hand furniture and no hope of finding a better apartment. Paris was in the throes of a severe economic crisis.

Mama and Papa were worried about my brother Max not having a Jewish education. All Jewish institutions in Paris were in complete disarray. We often wondered about what our future would be in France. Papa's sister lived in Pittsburgh, Pennsylvania. She had written to us, urging us to move to America, the "Golden Land." Because of the strict American quota system, only my parents and my youngest brother and sister, Max and Madeleine, could have moved there in the immediate future. They began applying for their visas. According to immigration rules, Claire and I would only be able to join them a few months later, since another relative would have to sponsor us.

One late afternoon, Mama came home with something she had purchased for me in a pawn shop. I eagerly opened the shiny, black leather case. When I lifted up the lid, I saw, lying inside, a lovely reddish violin. I took it out excitedly and held it under my chin, the way I had seen gypsies holding their violins in Dereczyn. Mama had not forgotten my dream of becoming a violinist!

We found a violin teacher in our neighborhood, Monsieur Dufour, who was willing to give me weekly lessons. He was of the old school: a strict taskmaster. "Mademoiselle Lew, let me tell you right away that you will never become a virtuoso violinist. You are beginning your violin studies far too late for that," he had said.

He showed me how to hold the violin correctly, and placed my fingers on the instrument to demonstrate the position. He gave me some technical exercises as homework assignments. "By practicing diligently, you will someday be able to play classical pieces," he'd said. I practiced the violin every evening after dinner and hoped that Monsieur Dufour would one day suggest a beautiful piece that I could learn to play.

While helping with household chores, I noticed one morning that I had developed a skin irritation caused by the harsh soap I used. Blisters appeared on the palms of my hands. They were not painful but were ugly to look at. I went to my violin lesson anyway, but tried to hide my skin condition from Monsieur Dufour.

My teacher told me to correct my hand position on the violin. Instead of obeying him, I tried to hide my blisters and held the violin slightly differently. Monsieur Dufour came up impatiently to me and reached for my hand. He corrected the position and noticed then the unsightly marks on my palm. "What is that?" he asked with a disgusted frown. I mumbled some words, embarrassed and too shy to explain what had happened. The lesson went badly after that. I left in a hurry and did not return for any more lessons. One day the violin disappeared from the house. I understood that my mother had returned the violin to the pawn shop.

Life intervened dramatically in the weeks that followed my last violin lesson.

Mama and Papa's visas arrived at last from the United States in April, 1948. We tearfully bid each other goodbye, not knowing when we would be together again. Jacques, Bernard, Claire, and I remained in our parents' apartment, on our own now to face the difficult decisions of our futures.

Shortly after Mama and Papa's departure, a letter arrived from Dr. Pugatz, the psychiatrist whom I had met briefly at the Soral camp, the one who had spoken to us about building a new Jewish nation in Palestine. This letter signed by Dr. Pugatz was from O.S.E., the Jewish social welfare organization, and it said that volunteer counselors were urgently needed to help orphans of the *Shoah* (calamity), the Hebrew term for Holocaust, who were arriving in France from many countries. These children would be housed temporarily near Paris. After they had made progress in recovering from their traumatic experiences, the children would be settling in Israel, where a new Jewish homeland was being created. The O.S.E. would provide volunteers with instruction in child psychology, Judaism and Zionism, and would cover all living expenses.

Without even thinking through all the consequences of my decision, I said "yes" in my mind, and went to see Dr. Pugatz in his office. He was of short stature, with a quiet, gentle voice. When he spoke, his words were very persuasive and they stirred me. I could see that he was a traditional Jew. Yet he was different from observant Jews I had known: he was the first psychiatrist I had ever met. As he began speaking, I began to think of what accepting this position would mean for me. I would be giving up my secure employment and a good salary. I would forfeit my opportunity to move to the United States with Claire when our visas arrived, and to be with Mama and Papa. Yet I knew instinctively from the moment I had walked into the office what my answer would be.

Along with other young volunteers like myself, I attended seminars on child psychology, Judaism, and Zionism. We studied Jewish traditions and holidays. We learned about the history of Zionism and about Israel's present-day struggle for independence.

Upon completion of these courses, we moved into a mansion near Paris, the Château de Malmaison, a former residence of Napoleon and Empress Josephine. There we encountered children from many different countries, all orphans, who spoke only their native languages. We managed somehow to communicate with them. French was taught during day classes, along with modern Hebrew.

Several months later, we moved with the children to Marseille, to help the youngsters prepare for their upcoming departure for Israel. We lived in a beautiful mansion overlooking the sea, called Villa Gaby. My sister Claire had by now already received her visa for the United States, and she was preparing to move there. She was dismayed that I had chosen not to leave with her. I knew, though, that I had made the right decision.

Many children were uncommunicative. Some were wild and unruly. Almost all of them had suffered traumatic experiences during the war. They had lost their parents and many relatives. The world was a terrifying, hostile place where evil forces went unchecked. One little girl of seven or eight, Leila, was from Morocco. The other counselors told me that she would not let anyone touch her. She would bite and shriek when any of them tried to give her a bath. She was thin and had shiny, black eyes that looked perpetually fearful. I was given the task of trying to tame her. I tried to hold her hand and she bit me hard. Then, forcefully, I undressed her and gave her a bath. It was very difficult, washing and shampooing her as I held her between my legs. I even managed to comb out her hair. Once she was clean, dressed, and combed, I pushed her in front of a mirror. She stopped crying and stared thoughtfully at her reflection. Leila then came up to me and began to follow me wherever I went. She wrapped her thin arms around my skirt and would not leave me for an instant.

My "twin" brother Jacques, like myself, was stirred by stories of Israel's struggle for independence. He knew that his job in the fur business would never satisfy his aspirations. He soon traded his old *maquis* uniform for a new one—Jacques, and many other young French Jewish volunteers, were all joining the Israeli army to fight for the new nation's independence.

The departure date for Israel was quickly approaching. I was excited and nervous about the future awaiting me. All the orphans at Villa Gaby, including Leila, were packing and completing their preparations for the voyage. Leila had become a smiling, sociable child who already knew some Hebrew words. The ship was moored in the old port of Marseille, held fast to the dock by heavy cables. Deep inside its hull, its wooden bunk beds would shortly be filled with human cargo: hundreds of children and counselors from many parts of Europe. When the ship cast off a few days later, I knew that I would be on the deck, and so would Leila, standing beside me.

EPILOGUE

MY ORIGINAL FAMILY of five girls and three boys is much smaller today, but enriched with a lot of nieces and nephews dispersed over three continents.

My parents settled in Pittsburgh, Pennsylvania, in a middle-class neighborhood across the street from the home of my father's married sister.

At the synagogue that sponsored my father to come to America and serve as its rabbi, he was given the honorable seat next to the Holy Ark. Since this honor came without a salary, he continued to work as a ritual slaughterer to earn a living.

Madeleine went to a secular school in the United States but Max went to a yeshiva.

At the time of his retirement, Father yearned to live the last years of his life in Israel. With their children's blessing, my parents moved there. Their final resting place is in B'nai Brak.

My sister Claire immigrated to America six months after our parents had arrived. She settled in Brooklyn, New York, with the help of one of our aunts. Soon after her arrival, a handsome young man, also a refugee from France, fell in love with her. They married. They have three children, a daughter and two sons, who now have children of their own.

My brother Bernard stayed in Paris for many years, and then joined my parents in the United States. He married a teacher from

Stamford, CT, my newly adopted hometown where I had settled when I first came to the US. We were neighbors and I saw him often. He learned to smile but not to laugh freely! I will never forget the last words he said to me from his sick bed. He said, "Thank you for coming." The next morning he was gone.

My brother Jacques stayed in Paris. He fell in love with a woman named Fanny, they got married, and then two beautiful children came along, a girl and a boy. Years later, Jacques decided to join the family in the United States, and rented an apartment close to where we lived. Then he went to work as a furrier in New York City. Later, Jacques died very suddenly from a ruptured appendix. The whole family was in shock for a long time. Fanny and her small children returned two months later to Paris, and later, moved to the suburbs of Paris, where Fanny still lives today. Her children are grown and are doing well. She is a happy grandmother of six.

My youngest sister Madeleine, a mother of four girls, is living in Brooklyn, New York. She has many loving grandchildren.

My sister Paulette and her husband, Maurice, lived happily in Paris after the war and owned a successful retail business. Paulette left this world a few years ago. Their son Michel, also a successful businessman, still lives in Paris. He is married to a woman named Rebecca and they have three adult children.

My oldest sister Hélène, whose husband was murdered in Auschwitz, remarried, but lost her second husband during a vacation trip in the south of France. A tire from their car blew out and he was ejected out of the car and killed on the hot, stony pavement. My sister was injured but recovered. She then moved from Nevers to Paris, where she became a successful businesswoman. Her daughter Simone graduated as a pharmacist and married a doctor. They have two children, Isabelle and Maurice. Today, Simone and her husband Jules are retired and the happy grandparents of five.

My baby brother Max, out of love and respect for our father, spent twelve years studying in various yeshivas and was ordained as an Orthodox rabbi. He also managed to attend college and to earn a Master's degree in English. Today, he enjoys retirement after teaching high school English in Brooklyn for over thirty years. He married a woman named Vicki; they have three children—one daughter and two sons. Their children are married now with children of their own. All of them are maintaining Jewish Orthodox homes. When I come to visit I have the pleasure of seeing a big, close, happy family.

Today this little brother of mine is like a big brother to me and the only one I have.

* * *

I look around me and I see with amazement so many changes. Professional women are everywhere: doctors, dentists, surgeons, veterinarians, psychiatrists, professors, scientists, presidents, Supreme Court justices, and virtuoso musicians. Not in my time, not in my family surroundings! Marriage and children, that was the destiny of most girls.

I am thinking and I am smiling to myself. Does that mean I am satisfied with my path in life?

I arrived in America in January 1957, after spending seven years in Israel, where I lived on a kibbutz and later worked as a secretary at the Berlitz School of Languages. I served in the Israeli army. Destiny was waiting for me in the United States — the man of my dreams was there, and he found me — we got married and produced two beautiful children, Rebecca and Gabriel, both married. I am now the happy grandmother of Jason, Danielle, Sela, and Matthew.

I love America, where I have felt free since the day I arrived. I am not afraid to travel and I have no need for identification papers stamped "Jew."

I have not forgotten the Nazi occupation in France, nor the Holocaust, nor what my family and I went through to survive. Nor did I forget my dream of playing the violin. Whenever I hear beautiful violin music, it always stirs my soul and brings tears to my eyes. But my old dream does not follow me daily.

What I do now is appreciate life, my family, my freedom.

It only takes a beautiful sunny day to make me happy.

—Sarah Lew Miller, March, 2012

FOR FURTHER READING

Adler, Jacques. *The Jews of Paris and the Final Solution*. New York: Oxford UP, 1987.

Allali, Jean-Pierre. *Les Habits neufs de l'antisémitisme*. Paris: Desclée de Brouwer, 2002.

Bédarida, Renée. *Les Catholiques dans la Guerre, 1939–1945: entre Vichy et la Résistance*. Paris: Hachette, 1998. 172–250.

Birnbaum, Pierre. "Anti-Semitism and Anticapitalism in Modern France." *The Jews in Modern France*. Eds. Frances Malino and Bernard Wasserstein. Hanover: UP of New England, 1985.

———. *Anti-Semitism in France*. Trans. Miriam Kochan. Basil: Blackwell, 1992.

Bleier, Inge Joseph and Gumpert, David E. *Inge: a girl's journey through Nazi Europe*. Grand Rapids: William B. Eerdmans, 2004.

Bourdrel, Philippe. *Histoire des juifs de France*. Tome II. Paris: Albin Michel, 1974.

Brustein, William. *Roots of Hate*. Cambridge: Cambridge UP, 2003.

Burrin, Philippe. *Ressentiment et apocalypse*. Paris: Seuil, 2004.

Carroll, James. *Constantine's Sword*. Boston: Houghton Mifflin, 2001.

Cointet, Michèle. *L'Église sous Vichy, 1940–1945: la repentance en question*. Paris: Perrin, 1998.

Comte, Madeleine. "De la conversion à la rencontre. Les religieuses de Notre-Dame de Sion, 1843–1986." *Archives juives* 35.1 (1er semestre, 2002) 102–119.

Comte, B., De Courtray, A., Dujardin, J. et al. "Les Théologiens lyonnais et la Persécution contre les Juifs." *Cahiers de l'Institut Catholique de Lyon* 25 (1994) 8–33.

Conan, Eric, and Henry Rousso. *Vichy: un Passé qui ne passe pas*. Paris: Fayard, 1994.

Coppa, Frank J. *The Papacy, the Jews, and the Holocaust*. Washington, D.C.: The Catholic University of America Press, 2006.

Cretzmeyer, Stacy. *Your Name is Renée: Ruth Kapp Hartz's Story as a Hidden Child*. New York: Oxford UP, 1999.

Delacampagne, Christian. "L'Antisémitisme en France, 1945–1993." *Histoire de l'antisémitisme, 1945–1993*. Ed. Léon Poliakov. Paris: Seuil, 1994. 121–164.

Finkielkraut, Alain. *Le Juif imaginaire*. Paris: Seuil, 1980.

Finzi, Roberto. *Anti-Semitism*. New York: Interlink, 1999.

Fontette, François de. *Sociologie de l'Antisémitisme*. Paris: Presses Universitaires de France, 1984.

Fouilloux, Etienne. *Les Chrétiens français entre crise et libération, 1937–1947*. Paris: Seuil, 1997.

Gildea, Robert. *Marianne in Chains: Everyday Life in the French Heartland under the German Occupation*. New York: Metropolitan, 2003.

Golsan, Richard J. *Vichy's Afterlife*. Lincoln: U of Nebraska P, 2000.

Griffiths, Richard. *The Use of Abuse*. Oxford: Berg, 1991.

Halls, W.D. *Politics, Society and Christianity in Vichy France*. Providence: Berg, 1995.

Hazan, Katy. *Les Orphelins de la Shoah*. Paris: Les Belles Lettres, 2000.

Hewlett, Nick. *Democracy in Modern France*. London: Continuum, 2003.

Isaac, Jules. *L'Enseignement du mépris*. Paris: Fasquelle, 1962.

"Jewish Children of France during World War II." Trans. Gerda Bikales. Livingston: Assoc. of Hidden Children of France, OSE-USA, Inc., 2003.

Katz, Steven T., Ed. *The Shtetl: New Evaluations*. New York: NYU Press, 2007.

Kertzer, David I. *The Popes against the Jews*. New York: Knopf, 2001.

Klarsfeld, Serge. *Le Calendrier de la persécution des Juifs, 1940–1944*. Paris: Assoc. des Fils et Filles des Déportés juifs de France, 1993.

Kofman, Sarah. *Rue Ordener, Rue Labat*. Trans. Ann Smock. Lincoln: U of Nebraska P, 1996.

Korsia, Haïm. *Etre Juif et Français: Jacob Kaplan, le rabbin de la république*. Paris: Privé, 2006.

Landes, David. S. "Two Cheers for Emancipation." *The Jews in Modern France*. Eds. Frances Malino and Bernard Wasserstein. Hanover: UP of New England, 1985. 290–297.

Latour, Anny. *The Jewish Resistance in France (1940–1944)*. Trans. Irene R. Ilton. New York: Holocaust, 1981.

Lazarus, Joyce Block. *Strangers and Sojourners: Jewish Identity in Contemporary Francophone Fiction*. New York: Peter Lang, 1999.

———. *In the Shadow of Vichy: the Finaly Affair*. New York: Peter Lang, 2008.

Lindemann, Albert S. *Anti-Semitism before the Holocaust*. New York: Longman, 2000.

Lobel, Anita. *No Pretty Pictures: a Child of War*. New York: Greenwillow, 1998.

Mendes-Flohr, Paul and Reinharz, Jehuda, Eds. *The Jew in the Modern World*. 2nd Edition. Oxford: Oxford UP, 1995.

Millman, Richard. *La Question juive entre les deux guerres*. Paris: Armand Colin, 1992.

Parry, D.L.L. and Pierre Girard. *France since 1800*. Oxford: Oxford UP, 2002. 185–201.

Phayer, Michael. *The Catholic Church and the Holocaust, 1930–1965*. Bloomington: Indiana UP, 2000. 176–225.

Rioux, Jean-Pierre. *La France de la quatrième république*. Tome II. Paris: Seuil, 1983.

Rousso, Henry. *The Vichy Syndrome*. Trans. Arthur Goldhammer. Cambridge: Harvard UP, 1991.

————. *The Haunting Past: History, Memory and Justice in Contemporary France*. Trans. Ralph Schoolcraft. Philadelphia: U of Pennsylvania P, 1998. Foreword, Ora Avni.

Sanchez, José M. *Pius XII and the Holocaust*. Washington, D.C.: Catholic University of America Press, 2002.

Sartre, Jean-Paul. *Réflexions sur la question juive*. Paris: Gallimard, 1954.

Schnapper, Dominique. *Jewish Identities in France*. Trans. Arthur Goldhammer. Chicago: Chicago UP, 1983.

Sciolino, Elaine and Jason Horowitz. "Saving Jewish Children, but at What Cost?" *New York Times* 9 Jan. 2005: 6A.

Séligmann, Françoise. *Liberté, quand tu nous tiens. . . .* Vol. 1. Paris: Fayard, 2000–2003. 319–339.

Suleiman, Susan. "The Jew in Jean-Paul Sartre's *Réflexions sur la question juive:* an Exercise in Historical Reading." *The Jew in the Text*. Eds. Linda Nochlin and Tamar Garb. London: Thames and Hudson, 1995. 201–218.

Szafran, Maurice. *Les Juifs dans la politique française de 1945 à nos jours*. Paris: Flammarion, 1990.

Vinen, Richard. *The Unfree French: Life under the Occupation*. New Haven: Yale UP, 2006.

Wasserstein, Bernard. *Vanishing Diaspora*. Cambridge: Harvard UP, 1996.

Weisbord, Robert G. and Wallace P. Sillanpoa. *The Chief Rabbi, the Pope and the Holocaust*. New Brunswick: Transaction, 1992.

Wigoder, Geoffrey. *Jewish-Christian Interfaith Relations*. Jerusalem: Institute of the World Jewish Congress, 1998.

————. *Jewish-Christian Relations since the Second World War.* Manchester: Manchester UP, 1988.

Winock, Michel. *La France et les juifs de 1789 à nos jours.* Paris: Seuil, 2004.

————. *Nationalism, Anti-Semitism and Fascism in France.* Trans. Jane Marie Todd. Stanford: Stanford UP, 1998.

Zuccotti, Susan. *The Holocaust, the French and the Jews.* New York: Basic Books, 1993.

ABOUT THE AUTHORS

 SARAH LEW MILLER was born in Dereczyn, Poland in 1926, to a large Orthodox Jewish family. After moving to France to escape poverty, her family of ten survived four years of German Occupation (1940–1944). She received her elementary school certificate in Paris in 1941, but was prevented from continuing her education by the Occupation. Through the help of a Jewish Resistance organization, Sarah Miller escaped to Switzerland in May, 1944 and remained there until the end of the war. While in Switzerland, she earned a pediatric nursing certificate. After Liberation, Sarah Miller was reunited with her family in Paris and worked for several years as a bookkeeper and secretary. In 1948, she served as a volunteer counselor for the O.S.E., a Jewish social welfare organization, helping orphans of the Shoah. She moved to Israel and lived there on her own until 1955, serving in the Israeli army and working as a secretary at the Berlitz

School of Languages. Sarah Miller settled in the United States in 1957, married and raised two children. She worked in accounting and financial services until her retirement and received several literary awards for her autobiographical writing.

JOYCE B. LAZARUS grew up in New York City and earned a Ph.D. in French at Harvard University. She is Professor Emerita in Modern Languages at Framingham State University, where she taught for thirty-nine years. In addition to numerous articles, she is the author of *Parole aux jeunes* (Heinle & Heinle, 1992), a literary and cultural reader, *Strangers and Sojourners: Jewish Identity in Contemporary Francophone Fiction* (Peter Lang, 1999) and *In the Shadow of Vichy: the Finaly Affair* (Peter Lang, 2008), an historical study. Her two most recent books deal with the German Occupation and its aftermath in France. She has lived in France and has traveled widely in Europe, Asia and the Americas. Joyce Lazarus enjoys choral singing, piano, and international folk dancing.

CPSIA information can be obtained at www.ICGtesting.com
Printed in the USA
LVOW101221010513

331727LV00005B/12/P